Published in June 2012

Copyright ©2012 by Richard R. Smith

All rights reserved. No part of this book may be used or reproduced in any manner whatsoever without written permission except in the case of brief quotes. For permissions contact:

www.richard@richardrsmith.com

Cover Designs created by W. Christopher Wanzie Copyright © 2012 W. Christopher Wanzie of WANZIE ARCANUM

Printed by CreateSpace, An Amazon.com Company

God Vs The Rest of Us:

My Journey into Healing

By Richard R. Smith

Acknowledgements

Grateful acknowledgement is made to the following for permission to reprint excerpts from the following works:

Alice Miller, "The Drama of the Gifted Child", Perseus Book Group, Copyright 1981 by Basic Books, Inc.

A Course in Miracles Copyright @ Foundation for Inner Peace 1975, 1985, 1992, & 1996 All rights reserved. Second edition by Viking Penguin, a division of Penguin Books USA, Inc.

RSV Old Testament, copyrighted 1952, © 1973, 1980 By the Division of Christian Education of the National Council of the Churches of Christ in the U.S.A

RSV New Testament, copyrighted 1946, © 1971, 1973 By the Division of Christian Education of the National Council of the Churches of Christ in the U.S.A

The sayings of Lao Tzu

The sayings of Buddha

The words and wisdom of Socrates

Thankful acknowledgement goes out to John Neale, who graciously provided his editorial services. John Neale has been a marketing media producer, director, and writer for over 30 years. After international study at Seoul National and Yonsei Universities in Seoul, Korea (1971-72), Mr. Neale earned his bachelor's degree in philosophy and history at Willamette University in 1976, and then pursued graduate study in film at San Francisco State University (1978-80). Mr. Neale currently resides in Fresno, California, where he works as Communications Director for a national logistics service provider.

Special thanks to W. Christopher Wanzie for his editorial comments and wonderful graphics art designs of the front and back covers. Mr. Wanzie is a visionary, abstract graphic artist based in Los Angeles, California, and is the CEO, Founder, & Creator of WANZIE ARCANUM, a company dedicated to creating abstract, graphic art for all facets of multimedia. His first collection of designs titled, "Clandestine Art", will be released to the public shortly. Mr. Wanzie is currently available for commissioned, customized original artwork, and freelance assignments. He can be reached at WanzieArcanum@gmail.com.

I'm grateful to the many readers that read the drafts and offered their thoughts and opinions.

Dedication

This book is dedicated to Lynn Rose and Arsen Marsoobian and all my WOW Factor friends. If you are fortunate in life, you will meet people like them. They showed me how I could get my life back and become the person I was always meant to be. They believed in me even when I didn't believe in myself.

Preface

In May 2010, I attended an event that immediately and forever changed my life. It was the most profound transformation I had ever experienced and since then, I've been trying to understand the meaning of that experience, how it came about, and to write about it. This book is the best way I can explain it. I hope I've done a good job.

What I know for sure is this; there is much more to us than we can imagine. Human beings are true mysteries of the universe and we're almost strangers to ourselves. My hope is that every single person in the world can experience what I experienced. It would change the world for the better as it has changed me. We are all connected in so many intricate ways, in an interdependent way that we are mostly unaware of.

My journey carried me deep into my heart and it became an adventure of emotional archeology and spiritual excavation as I discovered so many forgotten things I had abandoned long ago. Sooner or later we will all make that journey when the time is right and the right time will always be right now!

Namaste! Peace! Shalom!

Table of Contents

1   God Vs the Rest of Us

2   The Stent

3   Opening the Heart

4   Down the Rabbit Hole

5   Tender Moments

6   Divine Affirmation

7   Wonderment & Awe

8   Hypocrites, Liars, & Cowards

9   Living in the Kingdom

10   The WOW Factor

11   Dark Night of the Soul

12   The Myth of Jesus

13   GraceLand

14   Ayla and Her Mom

15   Killing the Jabberwocky

Introduction

With all the advancements in physics, mathematics, technology, astronomy, genomics, and medicine we find ourselves at the precipice of unlocking the mysteries of the universe. It seems we have arrived at the doorway of power over life and death creating machines with artificial intelligence with the eventual ability to download all of our knowledge and memories into a computer. Humankind has learned so much about our species and our place in the universe, and yet, we still know almost nothing about who we are as individuals. That riddle is left for each of us to scratch out for ourselves, discover who we are, and to decide the meaning of our life. It is a subjective verdict we render and if we don't do the work, we will remain a stranger to our own self. For all the questions and challenges in science, being human remains the greatest mystery in the universe.

Some believe that we are nothing more than nature's most recent adaptation to the environment, the next evolution of our DNA, and maybe the most complex biological expression in existence. Others have commented that since we are mostly comprised of stardust, we humans are simply the conscious part of the universe, or even believe that aliens left us here long ago. Most of us believe we are the children of a loving God, but we can't prove it!

The history of the world as written by men is our divine reference for all that we know or think we know. We have libraries of recorded events that document our accomplishments; the triumphs and tragedies of the combined prior efforts of all humankind. Most of these histories have been colored and filtered through the lens of the victors at any given time, so we will never know the full story of each conquest. Every history illustrates a collective story of where we have been as a civilization, as a species, but that knowledge does not have the same dynamic value and meaning as to what we have experienced in our living, breathing bodies. Stored knowledge is less vibrant than living in a human body in real time.

Every minute of every day the storehouse of human knowledge grows bigger, and yet we still have so many questions. New theories are emerging from ancient beliefs that are changing the very foundations of our sciences. Specifically, progress is being made in mathematics, cosmology, and a new science that investigates something called the "Akashic Field" or "Akashic Record", which may eventually evolve into a theory that explains everything. Mathematics, physics, medicine, and even history itself changes each day as new discoveries are made and ancient relics are uncovered. The truth is; what many people believe to be the truth about something may change radically with each new discovery. The truth is; as the collective body of human knowledge grows, the knowledge of what we don't know grows even larger. Every question we answer raises more questions. So this is the dilemma; the more we know the more we realize there is so much more we don't know. Understanding the dynamic ratio of the known versus the unknown is the beginning of true wisdom, and the sign at the entrance to the rabbit hole.

Sometimes life is strange and unpredictable, and we aren't so sure of our next move. Maybe its chance or Karma, when life itself seems to takes us in directions we never considered. It could be that we interpret everything based on an invisible set of rules from long ago. It is this dynamic reality of life, of a single, solitary life that has not been considered thoroughly. How is it possible to quantify the value of subjective human experience? How can we share a single experience with everyone else? How can we ever know for sure if we've had a good life? How do you measure that? How do we know what we know and know that we know it? These are questions for the theologians, for scientists, and psychologists.

Many of us have our own personal theory that explains what everything means and the truth is, each theory is a little different and a little bit the same. How do we ever really know other people? How do we ever really know ourselves? Some of us believe that we know who we are. We've already figured it out and found our authentic self, but we haven't. We've only settled for who we think we are and fooled ourselves into believing the persona we created is our real self instead of discovering the true and authentic person we really are.

For most of my life, I felt there was something wrong with me. Something was broken, but I could never put my finger on it. I spent most of my spare time and effort studying and searching for "the system" that would define me, heal me, and help me find my exact spot in the world. Searching and studying is what I do. Questioning everything is what I've learned to do. I haven't found anything outside Christianity that offers such a complete explanation of who I am and what my life means. Christianity helps me understand my place in the universe. I've studied Buddhism, Hinduism, Sufism, the western philosophers and many eastern philosophers, and while I appreciate what they teach, they never quite answered all the questions like Christianity does for me. What I now understand is that each one of us is a unique holographic fragment of the universe. It's interesting to me that when I reconnected with my authentic self I gained a "legitimacy of self" to all the other belief systems, even agnostics and atheists! Through the lens of my authentic self I began to better understand the priceless value of each single human life in the story of our history. How is it possible that each of us plays such a critical role in the grand scheme of human history? This concept seems fantastic, unfathomable, and crystal clear at the same time! I am only one person and such a small part of humanity. How can I ever make a difference? How can I matter at all in the history of the world? It becomes possible to understand when the perspective of the questioner changes from a general point of view to the experienced insight of a single life lived.

In *The Matrix*, Morpheus tells Neo that all he could promise him was the truth. My hope has been to find truth and meaning in my own life and to "know myself" as Socrates challenged us to do. The truth is, many years ago, each of us very carefully and cleverly hid our real self in a place we knew we would never ever return to willingly. My prayer is that you can discover and recognize your own truth in my collection of thoughts, ideas, and feelings. My hope is that I can share with you how I found my way home and maybe that can help you do the same. No one can do that for you, but we can help each other in our journey. We must each do the work for ourselves. With less than six degrees of separation between us it makes sense to say the whole world is depending upon you to find your authentic self. When you find your path in life, you will know what you were born to do. But the path will not appear until you are calm, clear, centered, and willing to accept what appears before you. Spend some time with yourself, examine what you believe to be true, and test it to see if it's real.

In *The Matrix*, Neo was "the one". Unlike the movie, each of us is "the one". We are all more interconnected than we imagine. Believe nothing you see, hear, or feel, but test everything to determine if it is real and true for you. I hope my words and ideas will help challenge you as I have been challenged, and then, dig deep inside and find what is there and witness it. You must want to begin the journey and believe that at some point you will find your extraordinary self, or you will never make the effort. You are "the one" and we are waiting for you to show up. We only ask for you to share your real self with us and show us who you are.

The problem is that we all need a little help and encouragement to step out into the light of our authentic self. All people need is just a very small amount of grace to make a difference; a small vote of confidence for them to find their real self. We are fragile and yet durable at the same time. Since we are all connected, we need you to bring your talents and gifts to us. You and I read about amazing people every day. We marvel at them and are inspired by their great achievements and what a single solitary person is able to do. What we find hard to believe, or don't believe at all, is that we too, are extraordinary people! If we don't learn to recognize the extraordinary in ourselves and nurture it, we will stay in the comfortable safety of our darkness, believing that is all we are. We find security in the obscurity of the crowd and will not risk sharing our unique priceless self with the world.

At some point in our journey we must be willing to step from the shadows of the false self, and become the authentic person we already are. If we don't, we will never get what we came for in this life. Many of us postpone the work of being fully human for a more convenient time, which sadly almost never comes.

The most convenient time is *now* because this present moment is all the time we ever have. The moment of now is when everything is created or ignored, decided or abandoned. Every person is meant to contribute their own perspective and talents to the collective whole and you are no different. Neither am I. I know that now and want to share what I've learned about me. The truth is that we each brought special gifts into the world. Every human being is a unique creation. There has never been anyone exactly like us and there never will be again. I am it and you are it and we are it together! If we play small and allow our authentic selves to remain hidden inside us, we will forfeit our shot at a real life, the human experience, and live our lives like ghosts passing in a hallway. We've all read stories of great people and envy their strength and courage. Each one of us has a great story to tell, and we need to hear yours, and I want to share my story with you.

Carl Jung proposed the concept that the whole human race may share one huge collective unconscious, and this collective unconscious makes up 90% of who we are, so we are all mostly one. In other words, if something is bothering you, then it's bothering me as well. If your dreams don't come true, then mine don't either. And it's deeper than that! If you don't bring your gifts to us and have the courage to share them with everybody, you will have decided to withhold a critical piece of the evolving universe from us. YOU will be the "missing" part of the universe. You are the one unique "key to the universe" for so many other people. Somehow, the collective expression of all humanity will be diminished by your lack of contribution. Think about the people who have deeply impacted you. Where did they come from? They clawed their way through the social structure and refused to be silenced or bought off by the current social values. They didn't settle for a pre-assigned place in the world, but chose to make their own history. At some point they believed in themselves, had the courage and faith to stand up, and share who they are with all of us. Who are you impacting? Are you ready to step out of the shadows and leave your own footprint on the journey?

Somewhere inside you is the power to influence the whole world. You don't need anything else. You already have everything you need. I was able to experience my true authentic self and now understand on a deeper level that each of us has a much higher potential for giving and sharing than I ever thought possible. It is almost limitless! This was the most extraordinary and unexpected gift I have ever received and I know the same gift is waiting for you right now. Are you living your dream or dreaming of a special day in the future when you can begin your life? If you are waiting for a special time, it is NOW! It is always now and not sometime in the future.

Many of the themes of my stories are Christian in content. I am a practicing Lutheran Christian and assume that many readers may not be Christian or Buddhist, or belong to any religion at all. The stories came from my heart, so they are true for me. They may not be true for you. I have tremendous respect for individuals and their personal belief systems. I believe the God I've come to know is big enough to deal with a little criticism, skepticism, and unbelief without defense or justification. I hope in your own journey you come to know Him.

I've chosen to share my thoughts with you one story or meditation at a time. Each chapter is essentially a separate story, but you will notice a common thread. Each story contains its own message, its own theme and focus. When I wrote them I was only thinking about my point(s) in each story. As I was writing them I had no central thread, no focused idea where I was going with my writing. I was only following my heart down a dark passage I knew I had to go through. Only when I finished writing several stories did I gain a perspective of the work as a whole. There are several recurring themes in each story. I hope they are helpful or at least entertaining. We are all really in this life thing together. Let me hear from you.

God Vs the Rest of Us

"I lie in the midst of lions that greedily devour the sons of men; their teeth are spears and arrows, their tongues sharp swords." Psalm 57:4

Most of us see God on one side of the equation and all the rest of us on the other side. For some people God is everything and for others He is nothing at all. There are believers and unbelievers and there are those with a scientific mind and others with no mind at all for such things. Truth is, many people aren't sure, don't care, or just don't take the time to ask the right questions. No matter what side of the equation we find ourselves on, almost everyone agrees, we are not God. God is something or someone other than our self, even if He exists only as an idea in our minds.

Most of us don't get serious about God until we start to get serious about ourselves. At some point in life we begin to question our value system. This usually happens when events and conditions take us down, when life itself seems to take our health, our money, or someone we love. We question who we are and how we got this way! We wonder, "How did it ever come to this? How did I end up the way I am?" How do I stop my suffering and struggle? Is there more to life than this?"

If we pursue the questions, we end up in a small white room with no distracting decorations and no magazines to read. We end up alone with ourselves waiting, with a small mirror. We end up trapped with ourselves and our boredom. We will always end up alone with ourselves when the illusion slows down, runs out of steam, and we can no longer support it. At precisely these moments it becomes possible for us to see the only exit left. It was always the only exit. We just never noticed it before. The answers to all our questions were always inside us. We never bothered to look for them there.

I've been skeptical about my Christian faith all along. That is to say, even though I believe in God, I find it hard to trust Him with my life. I still want to be in charge of everything. I'm not sure I'm important enough for God to bother with and well, I'm all I've got. I've read the teachings of Buddha, Confucius, Lao Tzu, Krishnamurti, Lama Anagarika Govinda, Socrates, John Locke, Rene Descartes, Benedict Spinoza, Freidrich Nietzsche, and the Bhagwan Rajneesh, not that I learned anything from them, but at least I've read them. These guys taught me to ask questions and so I'm always asking "Why"? I want to know the "why" of everything.

How did we all get here on this crazy planet together and what does it means to me and you? Are you a part of my reality, and am I a part of yours? How are we connected? Are we ever connected? I have a fundamental need to understand the many ways we are all connected as individuals. Is such a thing even possible? The whole world seems to be caught in a universal delusion and nobody knows the way out. Do we have any social responsibilities at all? Am I my brother's keeper? How do we make sense out of the meaning of our lives? I'm sensing that we live in a time when societies and nations are becoming "fluid", which is a new term for chaotic, out of control, and with no sense of direction. Anything is possible in the new era because everything is relative. What do we do when we see God on one side of the equation and us on the other side? How do we reconcile holiness and sin? How can we ever be fully and completely reunited with God? How can we co-exist with Him? Is evil only apparent evil, or, does evil exist apart from God? Is God real or did we invent Him? These are only the introductory questions when trying to balance the equation, trying to understand who God is and who we are. Many people today don't see a need to include God in their grand scheme of things, and many of us that do have a lot of questions, doubts, and concerns about who God really is.

As far as I can tell, the history of the world is a history of a series of conquests with one people overpowering another people. As a species our ambition seems to be conquering someone or something, bringing them into our control, under our power, and make them do our bidding for us. For all the glory of victory in the history of the world, it doesn't matter how many battles you win, how much money you make, how many diseases you cure, how many mountains you climb, or any other accomplishment if you don't know who you are! We may not even have the capacity to ever conquer ourselves, but we do have the ability to learn who we are as a person. We can get to know our self and to begin to understand our role in our town, our family, our nation. In the end, knowing our real self is all that ever matters! Never knowing our authentic self condemns us to a life of captivity, to ideas and values that are not our own. We simply pretend to be someone we are not and squander away the time of our life playing a role that is not who we are. And on some level, we all know we're doing this.

The world we live in is a violent place. People die every day in a million different ways. Some people are killed senselessly, some are killed in war, die of disease, from hunger, and very few from old age. It's always fascinating to observe people when they must deal with death. We choke on the meaning of death and how we dread it and celebrate it and what we do with the memories after someone dies. Every time someone we love dies, we are faced squarely with the list of cosmological questions: Is there a God? Is there a place where we all go after we die, or do we just go to sleep? Do we go nowhere? Did we come from nowhere? Where does the person we knew go? Is this it? Is there something else? What does it mean to be human?

The questions boil down to that one question: who am I? This is the question we answer even if we don't answer it. It is the basic question we must eventually answer with clear insight or drift away into an impersonal cosmos and live as a stranger to ourselves pretending we are someone we are not. At some point it becomes crucial to us to reveal our true self and let people see us for who we really are. Or else we live our whole life in a delusional state believing a lie about who we are and hiding behind the mask we made long ago.

Most people expect their life to be filled with hopes, dreams, and goals we assume will create a good life for us and our families. We've also experienced sadness, loneliness, isolation, and suffering. Why do we suffer and what does it mean? Is it necessary for so many people to suffer? Don't most people wonder about the existence and intent of a loving God when suffering is so widespread? Is suffering simply one of the conditions we need to experience to be fully human? How is it that some people experience periods of great suffering and survive them as a whole person, and become an even stronger person for the experience, while others are destroyed by their suffering? How can anybody ever think that any good can come from human suffering?

It is undeniable that people suffer. It seems for most of us, that's what we do. If we can find meaning for our troubles, we may be able to find hope and a way to not only survive, but flourish. We may be able to turn an evil into a good. And this is exactly where the idea of God becomes useful and where we can be open enough to allow God to come into our lives. It is precisely in our own suffering that we make the time to begin to work out the meaning of our lives. As much as we all hate to suffer and rush to save others from suffering, there is something to be said for the strength we develop as we struggle through problems and difficult situations in our lives.

The experience of a "Divine Presence", a connection to the "Ultimate Reality", cannot be conveyed by the crowd. It's a personal one-on-one encounter with our Maker. The divine connection is a one-on-one communion with each other in our shared suffering. It is a quiet moment, an almost solitary moment between two of us. It is the experience of connection, union, and wholeness. In such moments our suffering becomes known, becomes shared, has a name, and is transformed into the work of the soul. It is changed from an evil to a good. The work of being human is to learn to share ourselves honestly with every kindred spirit we encounter. It is in these tiny moments of sharing with someone that we may begin to actually get connected to the bigger world.

People are fascinating to talk to, to be with, and to spend time with. We humans are the deeper mysteries in the universe. The most meaningful experience of our life may be simply spending time with someone we love and sharing ourselves with them. Connecting with people is one of the secrets of the universe and human consciousness may be a new force in shaping the whole thing. When we get connected heart-to-heart with someone, the power flows and whole galaxies are created. It is this person-to-person connection that begins to reveal unknown secrets and mysteries of the ultimate. As we navigate through relationships and connections with others we begin to get a better sense of who we are and what we can do. The act of connecting with another human being creates a shared experience and a reflective pool that offers us a clear picture of ourselves. We do this with our hearts. It may be one of the most creative acts in the universe and may be the most profound act the universe is capable of performing through us. This shared communion may yet prove to be the next evolution of our species, the next step in the expressions of human consciousness, and a new understanding of our multi-dimensional universe.

There are almost seven billion people on the planet and each of us is a dynamic and powerful force for good or evil. We have all been pre-programmed from birth onward to do whatever it is we do. So far, we have had little conscious choice about this conditioning given our understanding of human growth and development. There must be some mechanism for self-examination, for self-discovery, for self-evaluation, and for self-correction. How do we find true north for our self? The goal for each of us seems to me, is to be happy, well-adjusted, fulfilling our potential, and to share who we are with the people around us.

I want nothing less than a full life where I can achieve my potential and share the experience of living each day with everyone around me in a way that lets me enrich their lives the way they enrich mine. If each of us could find our authentic self, the person we were born to be, that center of the universe that we are, and not the person our parents, family, friends, and society influenced us to be, we will experience a long forgotten freedom and sense of belonging and wholeness we may have never known or more correctly, don't remember. When we do this right, we suddenly find ourselves in a place of unlimited possibilities and endless resources. When this happened to me all the cosmic tumblers lined up and the vault door opened. I gained access to the secrets of the universe. They are all invisible and unspeakable. They can only be experienced personally to be fully understood and for us to develop ways to use this new meaning in a creative way.

The journey for us begins and ends deep in our own heart. What we discover there will reveal our own unique and forgotten truths. No one can do this for you. You must do this work for yourself, but you don't have to do it alone. What things have we already put there? How many situations have we already parked in our hearts forever because we couldn't cope with the meaning? How many traumas have we suffered through in dumb anguish not knowing what to do with the situation? How many emotional beatings have we taken as children when we couldn't speak and didn't have the vocabulary or intellect to understand what was going on and yet our souls recorded the events and we now suffer from their lingering effect? It is staggering! The whole adult human race swaggers from the cloud of the aftermath of childhood and we brush it off as nothing! We don't remember it! We are all such clever little survivors and we learned very early how to hide things from ourselves and not remember them ever. Once you get inside the vault, you will see for yourself and you will see yourself as you've never seen yourself before and also as you've always known yourself to be. It's paradoxical! It is an ineffable moment of realization that what is before you is your ancient and authentic self!

As adults we need to face the music and be willing to go deep into our own hearts. It serves no purpose to blame our life situation on our parents, our children, or anyone else. At some point in our life we must accept responsibility for who we are and the choices we make. At some point we forgive our parents, realize they did the best they could, and deal with the end result, which is us. We can then move forward from pain and suffering into healing and wholeness. It's mandatory that we become accountable for our situation. If we don't do this for ourselves, no one else will. No one else can! Making an examination of what is inside us is a job only we can do for ourselves. It's our responsibility to do this work. It will be worth the effort. Inside is a prize beyond price. Deep inside our hearts is our authentic self, and, when we find that real person, who we really are, everything in the universe lines up to empower us. We could do nothing as infants, as children, as adolescents, but as adults, we are free to take charge of the mission of discovery about who we really are.

When I first got inside my heart I immediately realized I had been the barrier all along. I can't blame anybody or anything. I did it to myself! Just like Dorothy wandering through Oz and crying to go home every step of the way only to find out in the end she could have gone home whenever she wanted to, I realized I could have changed at any time. I've been looking for a way in my whole life and every door that opened for me I told myself not to go in, until finally, someone just nudged me in the door and I was in. That person was Lynn Rose when I attended one of her WOW Factor events. That's all it took. But on this side of the looking glass we allow external barriers to influence internal drives and we quit on ourselves and so we don't try.

You have to try! I have to try! We have to make the effort to be, to discover our own Raison d' etre!

Love is so simple and yet my heart finds it impossible to create love let alone contain it for little more than brief periods of time. And when I get a few drops of love I'm never willing to share it. I need it for myself like oxygen in the next breath. I see now, in my stinginess, I deprive all those around me believing there is not enough love to go around or trying to extract it from others. One of the reasons for this dilemma is that I live mostly in my head, not in my heart. My belief system doesn't always produce the healthiest results. It almost never does.

When I got inside I intuitively understood that love is all there is. Everything else is a sideshow, an illusion. And God, oh yes God. He is everywhere all at once and I had the overwhelming feeling that I was exactly where I was supposed to be. And the Presence of the universe or God was right there with me as He has always been. Beyond that, there was nothing wrong with me. I was perfect! This was the complete opposite image I had of myself before going in. I was totally at peace and full of genuine unconditional love for everyone and everything. My consciousness melted into the fullness of the present moment. I simply became part of the moment and that was enough.

I also realized that there will never be heaven on earth. There is something inherent in the body of a human that sets us apart from everything else. It is a singular physical presence in time, an ego aware of itself as separate from everything else. These traits are hard-wired into us as a species and they also serve to isolate us from each other. Consciousness is the vehicle that overcomes the isolation. So we struggle and suffer in our singularity. This is the game we are meant to play in our lives. It is the struggle of the journey to wholeness, to oneness with everything else. It is learning to overcome our sense of singularity and find our place in the cosmos!

God, the real God, the Creator, comes to us and meets us in our hearts. Far from being the god of wrath, the god of the minds of frightened children, the real God is all about love. He has no choice in the matter. That's Who He is! The Bible says, "God is love." He is much bigger than what we imagined. We cannot see Him with our intellect and logic. We will never find His face in a microscope or a telescope. He can't be found in our successes or failures our careers or our fortunes, but He is there. When our lives get narrow and thin, when our breath comes short and struggled, when there is no more hope beating in us, He will come and save us. But it always seems to take that scenario. We must get to the end of ourselves and our own resources to get our minds right, to get ourselves in the proper frame of reference to understand, to accept. We are always on our knees when we meet God. Never, never, never will we throw down our pocketful of money and pipedreams and embrace Him. And no sooner than He saves us, than we will turn our backs on Him and declare ourselves in charge of everything. We liberate ourselves to a hell of our own creation and flounder when we discover we don't have the power to make it all work, to keep the illusion whole. We think God doesn't love us anymore or we think He never existed in the first place!

I find myself today, turning sixty, and looking back at the roads I've traveled. I was a hungry student studying philosophy, psychology, and literature craving to get to the bottom of the mystery. So many of my roads were dead ends and left me frustrated and confused. I've walked away from my faith and from God more than once, but I always come back. He finds a way to bring me back to Him. I know I don't deserve it. I'm never fully aware of the implications of the choices I make. They seem like a good idea at the time. It is always many years later when I can rest a little and begin to understand what the hell I did and wonder why I did that!

There are clear moments of self-discovery that unfold to form a bigger picture of life. There are also moments of rediscovery as we stumble into long abandoned rooms in our heart, places we had forgotten, places we need to return and revisit, to put our house in order. It is the work of the soul to accept the help and make the necessary repairs to give us a shot at living fully and authentically. It is in these tender moments of reconstruction and struggle and remembrance that we finally punch through the crusty layers of pain and find our true self. When we do there will be no need to explain who God is. It becomes clearly apparent He was there all along. And He was on our side the whole time. We just didn't see it that way.

The Stent

"Sometimes life is theater, a place where we can make an entrance onto the stage of our own choosing. There are times when chance intervenes in a way that reveals a complicated motive we've been working on unawares for a long time. It may be an experience for madmen only."-Richard R. Smith

I got my first stent when I was 58. It was a big one according to the cardiologist that stuck it in there. I watched the whole thing trusting the nurse probably knew what he's doing. I was calm until I saw the guide wire on the monitor and realized I was seeing my beating heart and the doctor fishing the wire through it! WOW! This guy was putting a stent in my heart! My beating heart throbbing away on the monitor and I am just watching the whole thing like it was a TV program. That was my first clue I could be in trouble.

The nurse said there would be a "little pain". A little pain is a euphemism for a lot of pain. It's one way of saying, "There's a freight train that's gonna run you over very soon." My body got real tense for a few seconds. This was the part where they blow up the balloon and smash all the plaque against the arterial wall of your heart to open it up so they can stuff the stent in there. I'm thinking that was the moment that it dawned on me what was happening. It was the moment I finally thought, "Hey, you could die from this thing!" That idea had not even remotely occurred to me throughout the whole heart attack I'd been going through for about three hours. A little light went on in my head and gave me pause to reflect on my situation.

Many hours later, a nurse came in and removed the shunt from my groin. She had to keep pressure on it for an hour to make sure it closed up properly. We sat there in the semi-darkness for an hour with her hand on my leg and her explaining what I needed to do after she left. She said, "When I remove my hand from your groin you must remain absolutely still for at least six hours. If you move, you might uncork the clot in your leg and you'll bleed out in about two minutes. If it starts bleeding, apply firm pressure and call for help. You'll have about two minutes." Those words gave me something to think about in the dark all night and to ponder the meaning of why I was still alive. After she left, I slipped into some kind of meditative trance and focused only on the breathe coming in and going out. I didn't move a muscle. *I didn't want to bleed out!*

And there I am again, back in my head, back in thinking mode. This whole painful episode was about my heart and I made the journey through it in my head. How do we strike a balance between the two? How do we intertwine our thoughts and feelings in a way that produces the existential creature experience that represents the full consciousness of the universe? I mean: how can we accurately and intelligently reflect on all that we witness and experience in this short solitary journey from cradle to grave? How do we savor our uniqueness and yet taste the flavor of the communion and oneness that is really all of us together? What is the magic formula for the head and heart to get synched up to produce the best possible life experience we can imagine? How does any 80 year span of life ever really accomplish anything at all? Maybe it doesn't. It could be that the history of us all is one long story of people that never got to live long enough. Maybe it takes hundreds of years to fully express ourselves as humans. Maybe it takes forever.

Maybe that's why we keep making the same old dumb mistakes generation after generation. By the time we get it right we're too old to move very much. All we can do is mouth a few silly things about how important our time is and Blah! Blah! Blah! We think Grandma and Grandpa have lost it.

It's funny to me that the stent restored the blood flow through my clogged artery. It kept me alive. It kept me going. It opened up more than my artery. It opened up an ancient chamber in my heart where I had dumped the garbage of my whole life. The stent cleared it out and removed the blockage so the stuff…the good stuff…….the real stuff…….whatever the spiritual equivalent of blood is, can flow once again through the veins of my soul. Is that just a metaphor or is it real? Is it love? Is it possible that love is the spiritual equivalent of blood for the body? Is this the blood flow restored to my physical brain so I can think or is it a heart pumping love through my soul so I can feel again? Now I'm not so sure if they aren't both real.

I am now much more aware of each moment in time and how I'm experiencing it. We are all only ever a few heartbeats away from not being here. We mostly don't think about it, expecting our hearts to keep on beating until what…… until forever? Hopefully until we can deliver our gifts to the people they were intended for, expecting to arrive at the beginning of act three in our lives on top of our game. What happens when that doesn't happen?

After all the festivities had died down and the guests and well-wishers had cleared out of my hospital room, I laid there in the dark adding up the cost for this whole thing and realized the curtain had just gone up on my own act three, and the only wardrobe change required was a little metal stent hidden very carefully in my heart.

The mystery and excitement of life is in discovering who we are and why we came here, and what we are being called to express in our authentic being. When we get it right there will be incredible energy flowing as we connect with others. If we don't do this, life sucks. If we're lucky, we get a wakeup call somewhere around the beginning of act three that teaches us to get busy with whatever the hell we were born to do.

The truth is, no matter what sides of the looking glass I find myself on, I always want to get to the other side. The instant I connect with the oneness, the collective unconsciousness, God, the universe…once I get to that center point of focus, the other side of the rainbow, I'm ready to run off in my body and live for a while someplace nice. I want to take that small glimpse of eternal clarity and gobble it up right now. I always have my own little plan for myself just in case God's plan doesn't work out. It's my backup plan if God gets too busy with other things. And when that doesn't work out, which after a while, it doesn't, I want back into the circle of eternal bliss where maybe I can get whole again. God waits patiently for my attention. He has forever. We have an average of 80 years to cram in the whole experience. Life is like taking your kids to Magic Mountain and as soon as they hit the gate, they're gone, until they want something, and then they're back. We're too busy doing stuff to spend time with God. He's waiting for each one of us to get to the end of ourselves, to let our curiosity run its course and run out of ambition, to ride all the rides in the park, so we can finally be together. It's only then that we even consider making time for Him. This process usually involves struggle, suffering, and several humiliating defeats and retreats before we're willing to throw in the towel. There is no easy exit from this place! Sooner or later we must all do the work of the soul. Some people never do.

And there is the gravity we all try to escape! Gaining enough velocity, enough centrifugal force to escape the pull of our past mistakes and misery and breaking into the brilliance of the present moment to be ourselves. But how do we shed all the weight and pull of the past, of the womb, our infancy, past the family dynamics and dysfunction? How do we outrun our karma? Where do we begin to attack the ghosts of yesterday that haunt us and stalk us every waking moment? We simply want our wounds to heal so we can go on living and yet, have no clue how to get healed up. We have no idea that we've spent our whole life spinning a protective cocoon where we can hide in relative safety from all the barbs and sharp words from those who claim to love us. It is always our loved ones that hurt us the most. We have given them the power and the keys to the kingdom of our hearts and they don't even wipe their feet on the mat before they come inside!

There are laws of physics and mathematical formulas that govern the universe and all the quarks, neutrinos, planets, stars, bosons, and galaxies. So where are the laws that govern us? What are they? How can we derive a mathematical certainty about everything we do, everything we are? We remain undefined and always in the superposition, never knowing which way we will go. What is our mathematical equation? Science and mathematics moves closer and closer each day to unveiling a new truth about the universe we live in. There is a concept in science that discusses something called the Akashic Record, which is a signature of information for everything that ever was. The theory goes on to describe the possibility that all physical matter is blessed with specific knowledge or information about itself and its relationship to the rest of the universe. The term they use to define the relationship is called "coherence'. How do we discover this "coherence"?

We turn to the ancient philosophers, theologians, and wise men from the East for our answers, but, we don't accept anything they have to say. Somehow in our modern world filled with all the new conveniences we no longer ask the right questions. We don't need the answers. We don't care about the answers. They are no longer relevant to our everyday life as they have no power to define us. The modern mind has become so self-absorbed that we define ourselves now in every narcissistic moment and who we are changes with our clothing. That works for a while as long as the merry-go-round keeps turning and we can keep the illusion in focus. Eventually, we slink back into our own heart, look deep down where we hid the grief and pain, and have to face the music. It's the only way out of our dilemma if we have the will and stamina and faith to take it. It is the journey of a single subjective lifetime.

I'm grateful for the intervention in my life of having a heart attack. That's what it took for me to get off the hamster wheel I created for myself. The metaphysical miracle of the stent is that it slowed me down enough to connect me with others heart to heart. I had to learn how to do this and the people that taught me, nurtured me, birthed me into this new way of being are brilliant and awesome souls. We all are! You are! How do we do it? How do we walk through the front gates of heaven and stand in the brilliant light and the very Glory of God? The gates were always open. They were always there right in front of us, but we were too busy, too pre-occupied with other things to notice. It's only when we slow down enough to hear our heartbeat and count each breath that we move through time at exactly the right speed to actually see such things. If you aren't conscious of each breathe, you aren't conscious!

It happens as if by itself, but it doesn't. There is intentionality, alignment of purpose, courage, truth, faith, hope, trust, and acceptance of each other, eyeball to eyeball, face to face, heart to heart, in a gaze that can last as long as you need it to. And there you are! The river of love and light and power will just start flowing. Let your heart and mind simply be in the moment and see them in front of you for who they really are; a perfect child of God, perfected by His love for each of us. I could barely do this simple exercise. I was scared, nervous, and felt exposed. All I could do was look back and pray and be thankful for these people sitting in front of me. Their brilliance and love and power illuminated every part of me. Their gaze reached deep into my heart into my very soul and touched me. When this happened I knew who I was and I knew them as they really are, as they have always been. When it happened, I became aware of the ancient wisdom I had forgotten long ago. These were precious moments out of time as if suspended in some other worldly place where beings are allowed to simply be and simply being has no other purpose than to be. We exist simultaneously as the one and the many. I experienced my waking self fully alive, fully aware with no judgments, no agenda, and no thought at all....only aware of myself and everyone around me. It's the place where God meets us face to face. And there He is again, the Eternal Presence of Mind or whatever you call Him. I call Him God. Everyone understands that!

On this side of the looking glass, each person is a unique expression of life and love, a one-of-a-kind blueprint for successful creation. Each one of us expands and contributes to the collective meaning of our species. On the other side, our uniqueness flows into one spirit and we become the One. I pray for us all every day and ask that each of us can find a way to get our hearts unblocked so we can all get connected heart to heart.

The world needs you and the gifts you bring to us. We need to experience your true, authentic self with all your flaws and brokenness, with all your beauty and brilliance. If you don't discover your authentic self and find the courage to reveal yourself, all the rest of us will suffer the poverty of not knowing you. If enough of us step out from our self-imposed shadows and open up, we will change this world. It is already happening now.

There is something divinely brilliant when you realize that each one of us, each human being, is a cosmic key that unlocks the secrets of a small part of the universe. We all need each other so much to live full and complete authentic lives, and, when we are authentic, we create an interlocking mosaic of life aware of itself. It becomes incumbent on each of us to discover the unconditional love inside us and share that with every single person we come in contact with. This is how we overcome true poverty in the world.

As I recovered from my heart attack and got used to the idea of having a stent in my heart, I was able to slow down and reflect on the things in life that really matter. I realize that I must be fully aware of the next breath I take or else I am not aware of the moment and the moment is all I ever get. Somehow I got so busy in my life chasing goals and deadlines that I just stopped living. I stopped being because I was too busy doing. The parts will all break down sooner or later and when they do, we discover that things are not as we thought them to be. Living in the moment, living breath to breath is all we ever get. It's up to each of us to make the most of it and determine what it means.

Opening the Heart

"You are the work of God, and His work is wholly lovable and wholly loving. This is how a man must think of himself in his heart, because of what he is. The forgiven are the means of the Atonement. Being filled with spirit, they forgive in return. Those who are released must join in releasing their brothers, for this is the plan of the Atonement." A Course in Miracles

We start by accepting our own portion of forgiveness.

Most of us live in our head, not our heart. Think of our head as the house we live in. We're very familiar in this space. We know all the rooms, all the nuances of this habitat. If our head is our house, the heart is the basement where we keep all the broken junk and other garbage. It is the place where we put the stuff we choose to ignore, the stuff we don't use every day. We rarely go down there, and when we do, it's only to drop off more junk. We've learned to keep all the bad stuff locked up in our hearts. Unfortunately, our very best memories are also trapped down there in the basement, right next to the garbage.

The human heart is bigger than we think it is. It is not just the small mechanical pump that keeps the blood flowing. It is also the center of feeling and the place where we store our emotions. It is the portal that connects us to eternity. It is a veritable mansion of rooms all filled with memories, feelings, smells, thoughts, and scenes from our life. It is a library of the data we've collected during our lifetime and maybe beyond. It is our own personal Akashic Record. The mystery of the heart is that we've crafted it to yield up only certain information, that is, only the stuff we allow ourselves to access and remember. But deep inside stuffed into room after room are memories we classified as top secret long ago. They were too painful to process, too hurtful to hang onto, and so our "little librarian" filed them away into one room or another, locked the door and threw away the key. Now they are gone forever, gone from all levels of consciousness, safely tucked away where they can no longer hurt us. But none of them ever go away. They linger on inside us.

The greatest task we will ever face is unlocking the volumes of mysteries abandoned and forgotten in our own heart. The secrets we've hidden away there over our entire lives contain the collective instructions of who we are. That information has been catalogued and filed under lock and key as long as we can remember. It's radioactive waste! It is also the Rosetta stone to understanding who we are and why we are here. The only problem is….we've learned to live with a closed up heart. We've learned to live in the shadows of our brilliance and survive on the scraps of acceptance from others. We learned to tolerate ourselves. Our world view is a grand illusion spun as if my magic, as if we chose it, as if we had the power to alter the fabric of our DNA and our socialization process. It tastes so natural and we drink it down without a second thought like medication that is good for us. We study and learn and reach for the dream crafted for us in this place and we think it's our dream. We've made ourselves believe the lie about who we are.

By the time we are born, we enter into a world we've been preparing to enter for nine months. We actually started before that, growing inside our mother's body, waiting to get out, and learning who we are and what we are. On the day we're born, we've already learned so much about ourselves through our mothers. There is a certain shock and sensation of being born into the world. Day one in this place yields an exciting separation and birth into our single perspective and uniqueness. The moment of birth is our grand entrance into a physical body, a place in the world, and the history of humankind. The die has been cast and the mold broken forever! The journey to immortality has begun. There has never been someone exactly like you or exactly like me on earth before. We are each a unique collection of DNA injected into the massive flow of human history at precisely this moment with a perspective and demeanor unknown in history. What will we do with our days on earth?

Psychologists tell us that by age two, we've downloaded the emotional programs we need to survive in this world. We've learned our place in the family, which becomes our place in the world. Each of us somehow selects the program that will shape who we will become and we begin the journey of maturation. The problem with all this living, growing, and socialization are the bumps and bruises and traumas we receive in the process. These are the experiential variables. They help craft our uniqueness into a distinct personality. By the time we are adults, many our hearts are closed off spaces we no longer visit willingly. We are vaguely aware of the general proximity of this organ, but we never do more than dance on the surface. We've already established a restricted access code so we can only visit under certain conditions. It is through this organ that our souls breathe the oxygen of eternity and learns to survive in this world. Of course I'm speaking about love. No wonder everyone is having heart attacks!

The very brilliant among us tell us that our experience of love is nothing more than a chemical substance that triggers synapses in the brain and causes us to release other chemicals in the brain and then we feel this love thing….or something like that. There is another explanation, a naïve, humble, inspirational explanation, an archaic, simple notion: That God created us to share His love in this world. Love flows through our heart into the world and into other hearts. God made us to be co-creators with Him to bring about His kingdom on earth. We participate in this process by what we do through the focus of conscious thought. Our minds may be the creative force the universe has been waiting for, but love is birthed into the world through the heart. Human consciousness may be the celestial change agent that affects everything. Lao Tzu said, *"To the mind that is still, the whole universe surrenders."*

What I mean is, in our consciousness, the universe decides what will be and what will not be. We each decide what will manifest into the world of man and what will remain dormant and secret for someone else to bring forth. We choose what we will birth into existence, what will manifest to others through us. This activity may be the cutting edge of physical reality and we each and all hold the key(s) to the future evolution of our universe. Scientists are finding out the deeper they go into quantum physics, quantum mechanics, and string theory, the more questions they have. What's most puzzling about what they are finding is the particles they are studying seem to "know" they are being measured, and behave differently than if they weren't being studied. Every new piece of knowledge answers a question, but creates a dozen new questions. This will go on forever. Bottom-line is we are created to channel love. God is love! Maybe in a few years the scientists will get the math right and we'll all be happy. Maybe in a few years, the Church will get it right and we can all begin to explore this universe and our place in it together. Maybe if enough people start living in the moment of "NOW" in their authentic selves, we can create a theory of everything that nurtures a fuller and healthier life experience for us all as human beings.

Somewhere in our childhood or along the path of our growing, someone closed our heart and hurt us and we never recovered. We learned to guard access to our heart. We learned that our survival and well-being relied on us keeping our heart close to us and closed to the outside. I'm learning how closed off my heart really is and I wouldn't have known except every Sunday, at church, it opens up and I start to remember everything. I remember all the hurts and sorrows of yesterday and all the small joys I had tucked away in there, locked up and forgotten. I'm remembering the little boy I used to be and wondering what happened to him. I'm grateful for God's strength to help me, to give me the courage to open up my heart, let the light in, the darkness out, so I can face my fears.

I imagine how hard it is for us to let our hearts just open up and let it all come out and let God in to do the healing. That's what needs to happen. We don't much want to do this, but it is necessary for our healing. Many Christians imagine what wonderful gifts we make for God and all He wants from us is a "yes". He gladly accepts all our pain, suffering, fears, doubts, and shame. Collecting our failures is what He does. He can actually help us with these things, but we choose instead to visit them on all those around us, who can do nothing with them. It takes courage to let your heart just open up and trust God to do His work in us. When we do, we become exposed and vulnerable. We lose control of everything and our fractured selves are exposed in this craziness. People can see us for who we really are and they may not like us. (Maybe we don't like who we have become) In faith, we embrace our nothingness and gain everything.

As we go deeper into our self, into our spirituality, our soul journey, sooner or later we stand in the presence of Truth. When we get there, we are not prepared for the experience. When it happened to me, I stood in a desert, naked and exposed to a brilliant searing light. The Truth is brighter than the light of the sun and since it is the Truth, It is undeniable. I witnessed Truth, stood in fear and trembling, and was burned up in the moment as the light just streamed through me as if I wasn't even there. I was consumed completely in a holy moment. When it was all over I realized I could never have imagined such a thing! Everything else I had ever feared simply disappeared as insignificant. There are no more human fears that compare with that fear! Of course it could have been only a chemical reaction in my perfectly clear waking brain. It could have been a hallucination or a bad dream. After that, I came back to my illusions and they no longer comforted me. They had become useless to me and if I still wanted them, I would need to pretend I still needed them.

We've learned to live in our head and our head connects us to this world. The head is the home of our ego and the thing that calculates everything. The head is the seat of our consciousness. Sometimes it works against the wisdom of the heart if we are not in alignment. Our hearts connect us to our real self, the person we left down the rabbit hole so long ago. If we try to live in our head while pursuing the needs of the heart, we will betray our true selves and settle for the admiration of people rather than serving God and our true self.

I have done this so much that I feel like Jonah. I've lived in the belly of the whale, kept my mouth shut, and gotten by. I've worn the mask I crafted so long ago to keep the secret of who I really am. I've gotten used to it. After a while, the mask doesn't come off. It's who I think I really am. My mask is the face I put on so people will smile at me and approve of me, maybe even like me. I've long since forgotten who the real me is. If we're lucky we get at least one trip to Wonderland and back to our beginning. On my way down the rabbit-hole, I left my mask behind, and when I popped out in Wonderland everyone there liked me anyway! It has been fifty years since anyone has seen my real face and the people around me didn't turn away in disgust, they didn't scorn or ridicule me. They recognized me! They embraced me! They loved me! That moment set me free from a lifetime of pretense, posturing, and game playing.

The faith journey we are all on will sooner or later require all that we have to offer, all that we brought into this world to share. Many of us hide in the crowd as long as possible, but the day comes when we must stand alone if we are ever to live as our authentic self. Some of us flow along in the current of life convincing ourselves that we are not that important, that no one will listen to us anyway, that it doesn't matter what we do. There is a time and moment when hiding is no longer possible. It's a day filled with mixed emotions; fear of exposure, fear of rejection, fear of our own failure, and the sense of a full heart flooded with love and knowing with confidence that He is with us. There is the experience of living in the truth and knowing that the last tidbit of our ego self is being burned out of us by the Holy Spirit and we are no more. This is what we hoped for, what we prayed for, and when it comes, we are reluctant to take the last few steps. It is in such moments standing in the brilliant light of Truth that we begin to comprehend those existential moments in our lives when all meaning flows together into a cogent whole, and for a moment, we understand the depth of God's grace for us and the hopelessness of going it alone. It is a series of moments when we clearly see the depth of our spiritual poverty and recognize our utter aloneness in this place, and how desperately we need God and His grace.

Many of us can only feebly accept this new understanding with broken hearts and be grateful. It's not much more than a crumb of truth that we scramble for and then don't know what to do with it once we get it. We can be a small light for others in the darkness of an uncertain world if we would but sit still and accept ourselves for who we are. Our lives will not work out the way we planned. Many of us fail to find our spiritual north, and so, we wander through our days not knowing our direction, not knowing the truth about who we are.

It is in this humble venue that seeds planted long ago begin to germinate and grow. God's glory begins to unfold in us and through us in ways we never imagined. It is enough to be forgiven and to be loved. It is more than enough. It's heaven! It's more than we ever imagined for ourselves. To know that we belong to God is the very beginning of the creative process and the knowledge of the value of being human. The Spirit works in us without ceasing, stripping everything from us that we do not need for the journey. With all our weakness and vanity, emotion and arrogance, understanding and reflection, limitedness and limitlessness, compassion and greed, we end up at the foot of the cross begging for forgiveness and living in the Grace that was prepared for us. It was where we were always meant to be. It is where Christ meets us in His forgiveness. It is where we trade in all our junk for His glory and purpose. It is where we become new creatures and know we belong to Him. It is in this place where we begin to know who we are and how valuable we are as a person. Only when we arrive at the end of our personal resources, talent, and experience, exhausted and spent, do we look for a helping hand. Knowing who we are and our true value equips us to become servants to all.

Imagine a world where no one ever stole anything. No more locks. No more keys. No more police. No more prisons. Why is the world this way? What is the mindset of the world that separates us from each other and divides the so-called wealth of the planet into the "haves" and "have-not"? How did we ever get to this place anyway? The perspective of life in this world is the result of a zero sum game. In a zero sum game, it is assumed that when someone wins, someone must lose. There can be no gain without an offsetting loss. Might makes right and power or the perception of power is the ruler. The perception of power in others creates fear in us. So many of us are caught in the gravitational pull of fear and as we orbit year after year through our lives, fear pulls us in every direction except the one direction we need to go in.

So how do we ever escape the gravity of fear? Love! Love is the opposite of fear. God is love. Fear is created in the mind, but consumed in the heart. Fear is ultimately not real, but is the product of the illusion of separation from God, from believing the truth. Fear is one of many illusions in the world. Choosing fear over love creates real consequences in our lives. When we run out of options, we must choose fear or love as the next step forward. We were never meant to live in this world without God. We were never meant to be so aware of ourselves without a strong connection with our Creator. We are not engineered for self-consciousness apart from God, and when we try to go it alone, we live as spiritual orphans. There is something alive in every human being; a soul, a spirit, an imagination, a dream. Apart from God, we are born premature, half-baked into this world. We have the capacity to imagine things that are unattainable in this world, but not without some help, not without some divine intervention. But that's what happened and we all see the results. There is no Great Society, no lofty idealistic goals that have been realized by any society. Not even in America does the dream find full expression. But we are not alone. We can connect up with each other and in that moment, God's light and purpose is revealed. We were always meant to be connected with each other. The Buddha teaches us, *"The way is not found in the sky. The way is in the heart."*

Opening the heart is a lifelong struggle. The minute we think we have it open full bore, it shuts down. I keep digging at my own heart and it always gives up more stuff. I dig harder thinking I'm getting to the bottom and more stuff comes out. I'm afraid I've forgotten all the little monsters that live in there, all the bad behavior, the fear of the dark, the embarrassment of being inept, the uncertainty of what would happen to my mom and my dad, and believing I could somehow protect my little brothers. I recognize an ancient aroma of rotting things like knowing I need to learn how to be brave, but being afraid. How do we learn to be brave? I thought it would be easier when I was bigger. It isn't! It's worse and now I need a bigger garbage bin to hide not only the fear of not being brave, but the shame of being afraid. And when I dig down to the shame, I open up the sewer where everything sits and waits and rots and smells. It is the worst of me and I not only live in fear that someone would see that part of me I don't even want to see it myself. I don't want to remember it, to relive it. I'm done with it, but I'm really not. It's still part of me. And so I don't. I put on the mask and pretend it never happened. I close the vault door and swear to myself I will never, never look inside again.

With that said, I begin the next phase of my life. This is the part where I start to slow boil and waste decades of my life living in the shadows and pretending I'm somebody I'm not. Not completely. There are elements of my true self, but only small embellishments that make the illusion seem real. I've convinced myself "this is who I am now" as if that's an answer. The problem with my persona, my invented self, is it's always only looking out for itself mostly. I'm not a mean person, but I am capable of doing mean things, insensitive things, of failing to be present when someone needs me. I can now only imagine the millions of time I could have made a difference in someone's life and I didn't, because I was preoccupied with my own self and the opportunity slipped by unknown.

Our parent's contempt taught us the craft of camouflage and we are now masters at making ourselves over into a perfectly lovable person. Mom and Dad never intended for this to happen. It has more to do with the process of parenting and the business of growing up as infants and small children and the way we assimilate information. Our true self is driven far underground and remains there until the day we decide to brave the dangers and go get it. It becomes our responsibility as we grow into adults to do this work of unwinding the myths we've accepted and woven into the reality of who we think we are. It is time to divine the truth about who we are.

The business of the heart is a dirty business, but it's necessary for healing, for salvation, for resurrection, and for rebirth. It is worth the journey, worth all the excavation required to get down to the bedrock of the soul, to where it all began. We find there are years of construction, layers of facades we've used and outgrown over the years. So many roles we've played and so many masks we've worn, we are not quite sure we remember how they all fit. They were always the new person we were trying to become and never quite perfected the role. We wore the mask for a while and then at some point, got tired of it, and traded it in for a new role, a new face, a new set of friends, a whole new social circle. Each time the mask grows heavier with the effort to keep the illusion alive. There is so much energy expended in building and maintaining the façade. It becomes a daily habit. We've done it for so long we don't know how far we've wandered from the main road. One day we realize we're lost! We don't even know who we are anymore. We don't remember why we do what we do; the ritual, the effort, the pretense, the expectation that our dream will come true, that we are just inches away from winning the whole thing and then it all slowly deflates and we move on to the next set of illusions.

In her book The Drama of the Gifted Child, Alice Miller writes:

> *"The child has a primary need to be regarded and respected as the person he really is at any given time, and as the center-the central actor-in his own activity. In contradistinction to drive wishes, we are speaking here of a need that is narcissistic, but nevertheless legitimate, and whose fulfillment is essential for the development of a healthy self-esteem."*

The battleground we fight on today was crafted years ago in our infancy. The stage has been set and the foundation of our character has already been poured in concrete. The struggle began long ago in our youth and we've already absorbed the first blows. It is incumbent upon each of us as adults to seek the truth about our authentic self no matter how big the rat's nest we have to enter. After all, it was the home we grew up in and the flavor of love we measured everything else by. Not that our parents were bad parents or family life was unhealthy. It is simply the way we are nurtured and raised. It is the flavor and texture of what we understand family life to be and within this context we frame ourselves, and our self-image emerges to cope. The only way we break away from our illusions is to allow the truth to come in, to witness it, to let it purge us of our illusions and falseness. This requires a shift in perception and a leap of faith.

Love is what our hearts are meant for. The heart is the organ that bridges the gap between heaven and earth, between now and eternity. It connects us to all that is and all that has ever been and all that will ever be. NOW is the next step and we are it! The heart pumps blood and oxygen to our physical bodies, but it is also the vessel where love flows into the world into another heart and creates a connection. God has chosen us to be His creative means to expand His creation of love and to allow His Presence to flow through us into this world. This honor falls to every human soul walking this earth no matter how mixed up or down trodden. We are all children of God. We all belong to Him. There is no distinction between the children who walk in His light and those still wandering in the shadow of the ego. They don't know who they are! God asks us to go and tell them who they are. He asks us to go and tell them they are loved. He asks us to go and love them for who they are just as He does. And mostly, we don't want to. We're afraid. We're busy. We're too important.

Opening our hearts to the power of the infinite is the most courageous thing we will ever do in this short life. It is a moment of truth where we declare ourselves to be who we are. It's the place where we encounter and face our most sinister demons. It is also the key to the universe. Jesus has already shown us the way. He has shown us the Father and we are already claimed and blessed and restored into His kingdom. Ephphatha! Be opened!

Down The Rabbit Hole

"What is described as depression and experienced as emptiness, futility, fear of impoverishment, and loneliness can often be recognized as the tragedy of the loss of the self, or alienation from the self, from which many suffer in our generation and society."- Alice Miller- "The Drama of the Gifted Child"

Driving south on highway 99 in early September, I notice the hoard of field workers as I pass vineyards and orchards realizing its harvest time in the San Joaquin Valley once again. This scene jogs faded memories of sights and sounds as the cool autumn morning air reassures me that the burning inferno of summer is losing its grip. The abundance of fruit and nut crops being harvested and gathered reminds me of the awesome production power of this valley. As I drive by the workers I'm suddenly filled with sadness at how disconnected I am now to this wonderful act of harvest time and the thousands of brilliant people that make food for us and the whole world. I remember harvest time in Fresno when I was a child and it seemed like everyone was involved one way or another in the harvest of grapes, cotton, melons, stone fruit, tomatoes, and figs. There was a small town flavor of Fresno. It's not like that here anymore. I had forgotten all of these things.

How many other things have I forgotten? How many meaningful moments have simply faded to black as I shifted gears through the decades chasing the dream and only now begin to access what has drifted downstream into the past? And where is this place I now find myself? What kind of a world do I call home now? It is no longer a simple place to live, to exist, to grow and prosper. The world I now live in is complicated, duplicitous, and only the clever survive. We leave very little to the imagination anymore. We have tamed the arid desert and the uninhabitable places of the earth and made them our home. We have harnessed water and technology and applied them to make the land to produce a predictable and abundant harvest right on time every time. It is now easy to eat, to drink, to relax, to scheme and plan. In the process we've created an even greater desert-the arid and hostile desert of indifference, apathy, lack of community, isolation, and political correctness. Life is so easy now. We've learned to survive in this place by becoming chameleons so much so that we don't even remember who we are anymore or where we came from or why we are here. What's the point? We just play the game. We get by. We survive. We scurry around like post-apocalypse cockroaches scratching for a stray crumb or two. At least that's what I do.

Every now and then something strange and exotic happens to me. I find myself someplace I never intended to be or even believed existed. When I came out of the rabbit hole I knew I was in Wonderland, but didn't know how I knew this. I found myself in a strange part of the forest, but not unfamiliar. As I walked along, the forest itself reached out and hugged me, pulling me along a predetermined path as if it wanted me to be somewhere. I came to a little clearing and there before me was a hollowed out tree stump smoldering with an ancient fire that had died ages ago, yet still remained alive. Deep in the trunk in a far corner I saw something I remembered, something from long ago, from another time. There in the shadows tucked down near a little hollow area in the trunk was a tiny figure of a boy. The moment I saw him my heart melted with grief and joy at the same time. My mind slipped back into eternity, I was burned up in a holy moment, and I see now where I had left myself so long ago, remembering, remembering, remembering….. I left you here one night so long ago when things were really bad and it wasn't safe for you to be there. I don't remember if it was something someone said or did. I only remember I left you here and then I heard him say, "I waited and waited, but nobody ever came back for me. I've been here ever since." I had no words for my real self. I was overwhelmed with shame for betraying myself, for abandoning myself so long ago. I had traded my authentic self for a phony persona because it seemed safe to do at the time.

Going down the rabbit hole takes many forms, but we all end up in Wonderland. It feels kind of weird and kind of familiar. It's the world I left so long ago. At first it seems like up is down, down is up. It's all backwards from the way I think. It's so peculiar like it was just yesterday, but I know it was a long time ago. Everything appears different than I remember, yet warmly familiar. I changed so much over time living in this other world. In Wonderland I am vibrant and alive. There is no need to be hopeful in this place-there is no need for hope as only the moment is real and everything in each moment is fully actualized or I should say, is fully actualizing, as it should be! Everything is what it appears to be and nothing more. The best part of Wonderland is seeing me in the looking glass. I am no longer that pathetic weak little broken person. What I see in the mirror now is a full, healthy, complete and real me, the real me I hid so long ago I can't remember when it happened. I know from the story that Alice belonged in Wonderland. It was her home. Can a story ever be real? Have I found the real me abandoned long ago in Wonderland or am I the real me? Or am I some strange blend of both worlds?

In Wonderland the lessons in the bible have a different meaning for me. They actually make sense! The stories and teachings give clear meaning to the reality I'm experiencing. I now understand that living in the linear starkness of the world those words kept my soul alive and gave me hope. And I realize too that Wonderland is something like the anteroom of heaven. For so many people living in the desert of this world, the stories of Jesus are just empty lifeless words, of stories for children and fools. For those who believe and hope because they have no more hope of their own, for those of us who realize our spiritual poverty, they are the words of life and of love. We cherish them and cling to them with desperation and hope.

In Wonderland being who you are is more important than what you do. Just being you makes you valuable, priceless, unique, and one of a kind. As Christians, we are called to celebrate each person's unique contribution to the Body of Christ and to recognize God's handiwork in each human being. Inside each of us is an authentic person trapped in guilt, held hostage by their past and afraid to come out into the light of truth. Jesus of Nazareth changed this by what he did and by what he continues to do every moment in time, but this is impossible to understand with our minds. It must be understood in our hearts. The trip down the rabbit hole delivers us back to a place in our childhood where we are free of the effects of upbringing, free of the negative images the mind has made, and free to embrace life in the heart. This is where we can see ourselves as the forgiven and adopted children of God, and know that life goes on beyond this world. You don't need any philosophy or theology in Wonderland. Everything is as it was meant to be from the beginning. The mind can always be fooled, but you can never fool a heart, even the heart of a small child.

I use Wonderland as a metaphor for that state of being where unconditional love is possible. In our present state where we live in our false self, unconditional love is a concept only. The masks we've chosen for ourselves prevent us from getting connected in any real sense with anyone without conforming to the script. Each of us is compelled to diligently play our role and then it can make sense. In the movie, "The Matrix", Morpheus tells Neo to pick the blue pill or the red pill. The blue pill takes him back into the Matrix and he will remember nothing. Nothing changes. Take the red pill and go down the rabbit hole and learn the truth. Neo takes the red pill and wakes up to the truth and understanding that all he has ever known is false. Much the same thing happens to us when we go down the rabbit hole and step into the brilliant light of our authentic selves. The red pill for us is to begin the work of the soul which starts with the excavation of the heart to see what we find there.

The rabbit-hole analogy became apparent to me when I learned about "poisonous pedagogy". This concept was introduced to me by Alice Miller in her book, *"For Your Own Good."* To survive this part of our lives, to understand it and make some sense of it, we necessarily develop a "false self" that helps us cope with our own differentiation process, the difficulties of our parents' personalities, and their unique relationship to us. We need them to survive! So we will do whatever it takes, even become a new person that solicits favor from them. We "become" their children, but that is not who we really are. The real you and me got buried with our parents' early disapproval of what we were doing at the time. The disapproval was not necessarily directed at who we are, but at that moment in time, we don't know the difference. So begins a life avoiding shame and hiding in the shadows of our parents' approval and then honing our skills to gain approval from everyone in our world. We find ourselves locked into the illusion of the matrix and that becomes our reality. Our "matrix" was created when we were children and we didn't know any different. We were learning to be "good".

From those early moments onward we forgot who we really are because that person could not help us survive in that place. We buried them deep inside someplace and only many years later, by some strange chance, by some coincidence, it may be possible for them to reemerge into a safer environment. We have to want that for them. We have to want that for ourselves and realize this is the way of the world. It is important for us to know that our authentic self is real, really exists, and waits buried deep inside with all the other things we've stuffed into that place in our hearts. There is so much pain and anguish stuffed in there, we fear to visit it, no matter what great treasure we may find there, even love.

Our trip down the rabbit hole delivers us to a safe place and to a time that is familiar to us. As adults back in Wonderland, we can now act in ways we could not the last time we were here. It's a healthy place of refuge and comfort. It's a place where we can see ourselves clearly in the looking glass and validate who we really are. We will approve and we will mourn for the loss of time our true selves have remained in hiding. In this place it becomes possible to consider the words of Jesus, to ponder the things above and to see God as Abba instead of the great judge and terror of the universe as he has been portrayed in the world we've lived in. The face of God for us will always be our father or mother until we are reunited with our authentic self. Only then is it possible for a clearer image of God to emerge.

It is in this place we can begin to better understand the true meaning of love and come to know that only love is real and everything else is false. We all want to do good things in the world and in our lives, but to be fully effective we must navigate the sub-routine of our personas. This requires us to dig deep and to have courage for what we find there. If our eyes are opened we recognize the many opportunities we have to screw things up, cause pain in others, and feel terribly guilty for being the bringer of pain. As we move forward there will be dark days and long treks through the valley of the shadow of death, but the trip is worth it. Hopefully we can use those times to better understand our own pain and suffering and allow God to heal us. He will.

I was the oldest male child and don't remember a time that I wasn't aware of my mom's suffering and struggle. It puts a burden on a young boy to measure up when it's not possible to measure up. I am so grateful for my great grandparents who gave me love and stability and let me be a child. When I was with them, which was often, I was able to be who I was and just enjoyed being alive. I think that gave me a leg up on my brothers who did not have that same relationship with our great grandparents. They did not have the same opportunity or historical resource. After all these years I have a soft spot for mother's without husbands because I know in my heart the depth of their concerns and how hard they must work each day to try and provide for their babies.

I am also aware how important it is for men to be the best husband they can be and to always be there for their children. Little boys need their dad to be there and teach them how to be strong and supportive men. And little girls need their dad more than the boys. I have been fortunate to have helped to raise three girls. I hope and pray that I helped them, that I was there for them, and helped them to learn how important they are. I hope I gave them some sense of security where they felt protected and safe. I will say that walking my daughter down the aisle when she married was the single greatest honor of my life. I have never felt more honored, humbled, and privileged than when I walked my daughter down the aisle and gave her away. It was another beautiful moment in my family's history.

I started out the first 20 years of my life as someone who didn't go to church. I made a personal decision during those years to not believe, to be agnostic, and sometimes I felt I was an atheist. I was actively opposed to Christianity and religion in general. In those days, I believed Christianity was a copout, a lie, a fairytale for the weak. It was an affront to me personally to see Christians coming out of church on Sunday and imagined them to feel they were better than the rest of us people. I felt inferior to them. I suspected they had something I didn't have. It would be many years later that I could finally understand what I had suspected was true.

When I finally made it to college, I fell in love with philosophy. After my first philosophy class, I knew how I wanted to spend my time learning. The constant philosophical questioning of everything carried over into my faith. The only problem is, all philosophy happens in the head and spiritual development happens in the heart. The result of these two influences on my life left me at war with myself for the past twenty years. I don't pretend to know anything, but I've come to believe that love has no equal value in the universe. If you don't have love, nothing else matters at all. I chose the path of the Christian, or more accurately, it chose me. The Christian faith is absurd! It is completely crazy and as the Apostle Paul says, *"For the word of the cross is folly to those who are perishing, but to us who are being saved it is the power of God, For it is written, I will destroy the wisdom of the wise, and the cleverness of the clever I will thwart."*

While there are many flavors of Christianity, most people outside the church view us as naïve, fanatical, foolish, arrogant, delusional, and self-righteous. No matter what brand of Christianity you practice, it's a well-known fact that if you don't have love, you've missed the message. It is only when Christians demonstrate unconditional love does the power of the message gets delivered from heart to heart. If we embrace unconditional love as the goal and believe this to be the truth, then we will be willing to be viewed as fools in this world. But we must always act from unconditional love or else we are the fools. The Great Commission is based on the experience of God's unconditional love for us. If we allow this love to transform us, it will shape and manifest in even the smallest acts we perform. If we are not willingly to risk doing whatever is required to connect with others, the message will never be delivered. It will fall on deaf ears or more correctly on empty hearts and skeptical minds. There is no fertile soil in such places for the gospel. The message of the living church on earth can only be shared heart to heart as the Holy Spirit flows through our hearts, not our minds, and we Christians must stand ready to sacrifice our religious piety and become the servant to all, especially to those whom we deem as unworthy. The unbelievers of the world are not the problem. The problem exists when Christians take the moral high ground and assume a sense of self-righteousness. It was the religious self-righteous that killed Jesus! I know! I'm one of them. Guilty as charged! I'm learning how unconditional love dissolves differences. Nothing else really matters that much.

I've learned that God loves all of us unconditionally. He needs each of us to accept His strength and to take the plunge to go deep into our hearts and recover our true selves. When we do we will see things differently than we do now. We will see with a filled up heart, a heart overflowing with love. Our selves will be fully affirmed and we can finally take our place in the world and deliver the gifts we were given at birth to deliver to those around us.

I fully accept my brokenness. I understand my feet of clay and my mortality. I am sorry. I can only now get down on my hands and knees and thank God for all that I have and know that it was all a gift. All living creatures will face death in the body. What I've learned is that there is a God that somehow makes all unbearable things bearable. This life of mine has been a divine gift, a moment in eternity for me to be, to be who I am. When I got to unwrap the present life God had given me, I was humbled and overwhelmed to find my authentic self and to see the "I am" that I am and to be connected to every living person through this I am-ness we call life. It is a profound moment of awareness when I am centered in my "oneness" with everything, and can simply rejoice in being. I can sense through my brokenness that at the center I am made whole in gratitude.

We all run headlong into our future, dying for it to get here, dying of expectation for what it brings, only to find our-self one day looking in the rearview mirror at our life. In that moment, it's all over. The game is over and we learn there is no tomorrow in this world. Everything that happens: happens now, right now! Going into the moment right now requires only that we become aware of our breathing. We are not the breath of the body, but only the moment before the breath and the moment after the breath. In that little space, "I am".

Tender Moments

"The meaning of our life is captured in a series of snapshots in time-those tender moments when we all seem to flow into each other and life becomes a banquet."-Richard R. Smith

Sitting at lunchtime in grammar school eating the sandwich my mom made for me before she went to work and thinking about how hard she works and how much I love her. I almost don't want to eat the sandwich. It was made with love and feeling like if I eat it, the love will be gone.

Lying in bed at sunup in the springtime and listening to the birds singing as the sun comes up and feeling the cool morning air as everything lights up around me and comes to life in a bird song.

Taking my children to school and watching them trundle off to their classes to face the another day in the world learning how to grow up and having to drive off to go to work and just wanting to take them home and spend the whole day with them and having time stop so none of us ever grow a minute older.

Lying in bed at night and asking God, "What am I going to do?"

Spending time with my dad shooting pistols on the side of the road and wondering why he was hanging out with me and never wondering if it was okay to shoot guns while cars were passing by about 20 feet away. And never thinking a seven year boy shouldn't be shooting a real gun. It seemed so natural!

Sitting on the front porch with my Grandpa and watching the sun go down. We didn't talk very much, mostly just sat there watching the sun go down and feeling the heat from the concrete radiate up. I was four then and maybe that's where I learned to "just be." It's the last memory I have of "being good enough'.

Starting grammar school every September and getting new school clothes that consisted of a new pair of Levi's, six white t-shirts, socks, tennis shoes, and underwear. This was the standard issue for me and my brothers. It was simple. Those were our good clothes. We couldn't play in them after school.

I remember going to Sunday dinners at my great grandparent's house with my mom, brothers, cousins, aunts and uncles. It was wonderful for us kids to all be together and to be kids. Our biggest challenge was not to break anything since there were always 4-6 boys and only one girl. The girl never got in trouble.

Being greeted by my two dogs and seeing how excited they are to see me and then realizing that after the tail-wagging and face-licking hellos, they know they're going to get a treat. Hummmm! Unconditional love? Absolutely, but the treats don't hurt.

Having my daughter put my hand on her belly to feel the baby move for the first time and knowing her future is moving around in there rearranging the furniture with her little hands and feet, so to speak.

Watching my mom iron our clothes and sighing a lot and knowing she was trying to work out our futures while she was ironing.

Walking my daughter down the aisle and having it be the happiest day of my life and knowing I was doing the most important thing I had ever done! A man doesn't see that sort of thing coming.

Trying frantically to glue all the broken pieces of my life back together and having none of them fit, none of them staying together, and then giving up completely, knowing I can't do this, then watching as grace flows into my brokenness and puts all the pieces exactly where they belong. WOW!

Looking into someone's eyes and seeing their beautiful, brilliant, soul and then seeing Christ and then seeing my forgiven self. I see the little boy that I was so many years ago and realize that we are all truly in God every single day of our life. We mostly don't know it.

Standing over the floor furnace when I was young and feeling the heat rising up out of the floor and warming my body. There's nothing like getting out of bed on a cold winter morning to get ready for school. My brothers and I would just stand there shivering and warming up and mustering up enough courage and warmth to go into the kitchen to get a cup of coffee.

Waking up in the morning in bed and wondering how I got there when I was four. And then waking up in bed when I was 34 and wondering how I got there. Some things never change!

I remember the looks in my brother's eyes when I told them our mother was dead. It was terrible. There are times when my mere mortality is unbearable and all I can do is hang on. I could do nothing except be there and cry with them. Sometimes being a big brother is no help at all.

Feeling an overwhelming wave of gratitude just before Thanksgiving and making a fire in the fireplace and watching the rain and being with my family for a couple of days. It's so cozy and magical sitting by the fireplace on a cold rainy day and soaking in the warmth of the fire and being a family.

Looking at the color of the night sky in winter- it looks black, but it's really an incredible inky blue.

Witnessing the strength, love and patience in my daughter as she gave birth to her baby and then, holding my two hour old granddaughter in my arms and I didn't break her. Babies are really rugged!

Standing in the middle of a vacant lot with my friends and shooting an arrow straight up in the air and watching it disappear into the sky.... And then everyone runs in all directions waiting for the arrow to land. It's what boys do and men do for that matter. We'd do it right now if somebody had a bow and arrow.

Imagining myself lying in bed on the last day of my life and being overwhelmed with gratitude for my extraordinary life and being humbled by how much I've been loved and how much I have loved others. Somehow I know that when tomorrow comes and only my body is left here, I will still be connected to every single heart I'm connected with now. I will be in a place of profound peace and reunited with everyone that has gone before me. I call that place heaven.

There is something that happens throughout our life when we experience these magical moments with family and friends and we simply want time to stop. Somehow things come together in that instant and life is perfect. The fullness of the moment will never be sweeter, never be better than right now, when the whole universe becomes a symphony. We hold it tight in our hearts and capture it, only to reluctantly see it drift downstream as time flows on, the sun goes down, and we must all keep moving.

Experiencing such moments and savoring their meaning cause me to wonder why life isn't always this way. These magical moments are flashes of enlightenment, harmony, the cohesive expression of sharing and togetherness when we are all connected. As hard as we try to create such moments, they seem to just happen on their own and then they evaporate into the air around us.

At these times I know love is real and can never be destroyed, never erased, never buried or burned up, and must go on forever. If I'm paying attention, I catch a glimpse of myself learning something and I realize how much I don't know. It is a simple joy to behold the brilliant mystery of life ever-unfolding each moment of each day. In these tender moments my very breath comes in and goes out in slow measured acts of affirmation, my heart beats with a timeless sound and my prayer becomes pure and holy. All pretense is gone and I am reduced to a silent witness humbled by the beauty of the moment and grateful to be part of it. I am! In these moments I hold everyone close to my heart and soul and protect them from all harm in a simple prayer. In these moments I realize the depth of my spiritual poverty and am surprised to unwrap the brilliant presents that God has given me. It is a bitter sweet joy to know "I too am loved."

In His infinite wisdom He lets me experience the sweet agony of moving through time, to manage it, to get lost in it, and to navigate it to His purpose, and then, to see it drain away one day at a time. It is toil and struggle, heartbreak and joy, faith and faithless, and in the end, I win the kingdom through grace alone. There are moments in time when we see with great clarity the precarious situation of being human.

The moment we are born the clock starts running and we have only so much time to understand the meaning of our days if we ever do at all. At some point I became aware I could not stop the constant advance of time, and while I can imagine a multitude of potential scenarios for my life, I know I don't have any power to change the course of events that will extinguish it. I can only hang on, make intelligent choices, and wait for the inevitable. My hope is to make a small difference in someone's life.

There are times when we lock onto a gaze from a stranger and in an instant we share a knowing look, a shared moment of recognizing each other from another time. It happens when we see a photo of someone struggling or suffering or dying that sends a laser arrow right through our heart and jolts us and connects us up with all the pain of a broken humanity. We understand that for all the modern conveniences, people are the same as they have always been. It doesn't matter what nationality, what sex, what age, young or old, we are all the same. We are all exactly the same being. With a modest amount of meditation our heart reveals that we are all really one person.

It seems to me that as we gather and collect these tender moments they have the power to define who we are in the world. They become treasures we collect on our life journey and remain frozen moments in time that consist of a smell, a sound, a glance, a feeling, a suspended moment of clarity we cling to. Mostly we cannot fabricate these moments. They just happen on their own-they appear, they are meant to be in that moment, and then are gone. These are the little trophies God collects and keeps for us in heaven when we arrive.

Every single time I realize I'm in the middle of a tender moment, I have exactly the same thought: the meaning of the moment lives forever. It will not diminish. It has been crocheted into the fabric of our collective hearts and preserved in that place we call heaven. It is not possible for such profound meaning to happen and then dissipate into nothingness.

At the very end of our days we will only remember the tender moments. It's a pity we consume so much of our time every day with trivial details that won't ever really matter, but which we must all attend to. Apart from being an annoyance and distraction, these moments should serve as motivation for us all to a heightened sense of awareness for those tender moments. With a little practice, everything we do becomes a tender moment. When that happens I will know I've arrived!

Divine Affirmation

"Ask not to be forgiven, for this has already been accomplished. Ask, rather, to learn how to forgive, and to restore what always was to your unforgiving mind. Atonement becomes real and visible to those who use it. On earth this is your only function, and you must learn that it is all you want to learn. You will feel guilty till you learn this."
-A Course in Miracles

Standing in line at the grocery store, I become aware of my growing anxiety, realizing it will not get me through the checkout counter any faster. I relax and enjoy the moment of just being with a group of people that will never come together again. Suddenly I am aware that everyone around me is in a hurry. I see concern and tension in their faces as they fall farther behind on their task lists. I flash a calm welcoming smile, and pretty soon one or two people smile back at me, affirming our common dilemma, and silently acknowledging we aren't going anywhere soon. I'd like to think we made a small connection and shared a wasted moment together.

Maybe it wasn't meaningless. Maybe all we ever really need is a smile from a stranger, or, God forbid, a friend. Maybe that's the only moment that ever really counts. Maybe our whole life is spent standing in a cosmic checkout line. What's in my shopping cart? What did I value with the time of my life?

It's difficult to focus on the meaning of a moment, a glance, a conversation or anything because we are so busy and life is flowing by like a raging river. We live in a demanding world and we must all multi-task to keep up or, or, or what? What if we just stopped multi-tasking? What would happen? Probably nothing would happen.

With all the things we're getting done, you'd think we'd feel special and important, but we don't. We're behind. We're desperate. One by one, we've seen our dreams slide out of reach of our imaginations beyond the influence of our hearts. They just drift away, leaving us alone with this "stuff" we do. We're afraid of falling behind. What we need is a dose of divine affirmation, but how do we get it? Where do we go and who do we see for a divine affirmation? Are they real? How long do they last? Does it hurt when you get one?

Looking into the eyes of another person for long periods of time without saying a word is one way. It works! When human beings communicate, only 7% of the message is communicated with language. The other 93% of the message is non-verbal or something like that. Maybe it's 10% verbal or 15%, but the meaning is mostly non-verbal, so content is less important than showing up in person and being who you are. Being with someone is much more important than whatever words we speak. There is so much I don't understand about mere physical presence, about being with someone fully, completely, and actually sharing a moment together. I'm learning that talking is less important than just being there in a shared moment.

When I looked into the eyes of strangers as part of my training, several extraordinary things happened: I could see the person's soul and spirit. I saw them as they really are. I saw them as the perfect creatures God made them to be! It's the most beautiful communion imaginable, to see people from a perspective without judgment, lovingly accepting them for who they are. But what happened next was unimaginable. It was another miraculous event I never expected. What happened next was, I saw the person looking back at me and somehow, I saw a reflection of myself in their face as they must have been seeing me. I saw myself as God intended me to be! I saw myself without self-criticism or judgment and remembered a moment in time long ago when I was that person because I didn't know any better.

In that moment I felt like God was looking in on me and giving me a divine affirmation. This was a gift I never, ever expected to see this side of heaven. Immediately I understood the power of my adoption and the plan God has for me. I understand the sacrifice Jesus made for me and I'm standing in the brilliant light of heaven. Then I realized these gifts are meant for every single person when they choose to acknowledge them.

Words are such a pathetically poor medium of communication. There are some aspects of being human that are ineffable, inexpressible, and we do well to silently witness the experiences and allow them to change us and mold us into more complete creatures.

Unconditional love is what God does. Conditional love is what we do in our own power. Conditional love is the best we can do by ourselves. People will read these words and think, "Not me!" Think for a moment about the people in your life and then think about the people you enjoy being around. Now think of those people you know that just drive you crazy. If you can make that distinction your vision is too shallow. And there you are. Conditional love! People have to be nice to us and then we can love them. Many of the people we bring into our lives are assigned a role we need them to play. We select them and script them so their "character" conforms to the role we need them to play in our little drama so it can play out the way we need it to for us to live happily ever after, or so we think. If they do a good job with their part, we reward them by "loving" them. We love them for what they do, not for who they are. It's a quid pro quo kind of love. Quid pro quo is the currency of this world.

For many of us, unconditional love is an idea only. It's a general theory, a hypothesis, and lives only in our head where it's not real. We can experience unconditional love anytime we're ready to take the plunge. All we have to do is look into someone's eyes and be open to whatever experience happens in the shared moment. That moment is all there really is and all the other things in our life fade to black as small details. We can let go anytime we want and make the intimate connection. We just don't want to. We don't want to risk exposing our vulnerable self.

Instead, we cling to our opinions and prejudices and judgments to navigate us around the intimacy of the connection. God made the connection between us the real destination! It is in the act of one on one intimate connection when our hearts are open that we may discover the kingdom of heaven and our sacred oneness.

There are so many of us who go to church, read our bibles faithfully, and pray for everyone. We keep the faith as best we can and sometimes it seems that nothing really changes, that we aren't making any difference at all. But a change happens when we connect up with people in an intimate personal way. The problem is we hesitate to put all the chips on the table. We hold back from engaging too much for fear we will get too close for comfort, reveal our smallness, our ugly side, our weaknesses, our flaws. These are the character scars that remain long after the damage has been done. We've all got them. They are the medals and ribbons of our imperfect brilliance!

Many successful people have learned to use their flaws as a way to connect with people. The truth is most of our flaws are the very things that endear us to so many people around us. They make us human and vulnerable. They require us to struggle and measure up. They present us with interior obstacles for us to overcome. It's the stuff God needs to do what He does. Those bonds born out of necessity from pain, suffering, neglect, poverty and ignorance all serve to pull us together into a single beating heart for a common cause.

When I was in first grade and we were learning to read, our teacher made us stand by our desks and read to the class. The first time I did this, I got stuck on a word. I didn't know the word. I couldn't sound it out, so I just looked at her like, "I'm stuck here." She was very kind. She said, "What is the word." I said, "I don't know." And she said, "No, 'what' is the word." The whole time the class was giggling and laughing. The word I didn't recognize was "what." She was telling me the word in a statement, but I was hearing it as a question I could not answer. It was embarrassing for me to be the only one that didn't know what everyone was laughing about. I was the only one that wasn't getting the joke. It was as if they were all laughing at me. It was as if I was the joke. That's a feeling that's stuck with me. Whenever I speak publicly I have to overcome the fear of the audience laughing at me.

I'm certain that most of us have experienced moments like this and they silently block us. They erect a barrier somewhere inside us that inhibits our growth. We simply stop growing in that direction, refusing to risk any further embarrassment or allow ourselves to be in the same position again. So when I get up in front of people, I worry they will laugh at me for no apparent reason and that I'll be the only one that doesn't know the joke.

That's just one example of the blocks that get thrown our way as we develop into who we are supposed to be. I'm sure we can all think of many other examples of single incidents that shape our growth, create fear, pain, and anxiety for the rest of our lives. We get so stuffed up, so blocked up, we begin to stagnate. We become isolated and on some level, we begin to slowly die.

If you study the people around you, you'll notice how little some of them actually risk. They don't reveal much about themselves. Maybe you've known them for years and what do you really know about them? They aren't sure who they are anymore so they stay closed up and cut off and safe from any actual sharing. We all have the potential to disconnect, to close ourselves off from everybody else, and withdraw into our own little shelter.

A divine affirmation is needed. An intervention with sufficient intensity to snap us out of our perpetual daydream and slap us back into some sense of healthy authentic being. Over time, we've molded ourselves to fit the people and environment around us. People fit in wherever they are. They join the team, even reluctantly, but they join. It may be our job. It may be Little League. It may even be our marriage. Group dynamics takes over and we start conforming to the group normal. In the process, we squirrel away whole chucks of our authentic self like a dog hiding a bone. "I'll come back for that later when I'm real hungry", we think, and we never do. And then one day we wake up and can't remember where we buried ourselves.

We wake up lost in the world, alone with no moral compass, no sense of direction, no place to call home. We join the hundreds of millions of other lost souls marching through the day, waiting for the weekend, for payday, vacation, retirement, and wondering how it all ends, hoping to find our way back home. The disconnection can come from anywhere, from being tired, from being desperate, or just plain giving up for a while. When that happens, we simply drift downstream hoping to catch our breath so we can return to the arena and fight some more.

Home for us is and has always been our authentic self. If we are willing to spend more than a moment or quick glance at the stranger in the mirror, we can begin the process of reconnecting with our self. It requires honesty, courage, and faith to come to terms with the creature that stares back at us. This self-image is our own creation, our persona, our mask, the ghost of what we thought we were. God has not left us alone in this place. He can't leave us alone. We're part of Him. We're His children.

The distinction of human existence is the experience of consciousness, of awareness in the form of a physical body, and a sense of separation from our life source, from God. It's easy to slide into isolation and loneliness and once there, learn to accept some level of it as a constant companion, as a fact of life. As creatures we were never meant to exist in isolation. We are meant to live in community with others. This is only one of the many disappointments and dysfunctions we accept for ourselves and they become who we are-part of the expression of ourselves and the way we cope with ourselves and our relationships.

Alice Miller, in her book, *The Drama of the Gifted Child* says, *"If a person is able, during this long process, to experience that he never was 'loved 'as a child for what he was but for his achievements, success and good qualities, and that he sacrificed his childhood for this "love", this will shake him very deeply but one day he will feel the desire to end this courtship. He will discover in himself a need to live according to his "true self" and no longer be forced to earn love, a love that at root, still leaves him empty-*

handed since it is given to the "false self", which he has begun to relinquish."

This realization, painful as it is, leaves us stunned but hopeful. People now have a face for our pain, for our suffering. We now slowly begin to understand what kind of things went wrong and the ancient forces that shaped and molded our brokenness. We can now begin to heal, to get whole. People do this in many ways as they begin to see themselves as part of something bigger than themselves. Many people join organizations they believe in and become active members advancing their cause. For me, I found my authentic self in God. For lack of a better explanation, God saved me. He saves me again and again and again. He saves me every single day and every moment of every day. I don't care how He does it. I just know it works for me. I know from experience that when I get centered, when the waters of my soul are calm and still, like a mirror, I can hear His "still small voice" and realize He has never stopped talking to me, never stopped being with me, never stopped loving me. I was just too busy with the noise in my life to listen or hear Him.

If we are willing to sit still, turn off the atomic clock, focus on our breathing and disconnect all thoughts and just be present in quiet contemplation, in silent witness to all that is around us, God will come to us and we will know that He is! If we stay there long enough, we experience a quiet and profound peace that absorbs us into its Presence. Call it God, Jesus, Buddha, the Force, the Great Spirit, Nirvana, Satori, Heaven, or the Space of the Creative Edge of The Universe, or whatever. It is in this quiet space where we learn a new language, an eternal song, an ancient fragrance, and begin to remember who we are. We can understand ourselves with a new wisdom, a new light of being, and begin to 'remember' that person we used to be so long ago.

Science is now theorizing a connection between everything. They call it "coherence". Coherence is that invisible force that connects everything to everything else. We haven't seen it. We can't actually prove it, but we know it exists. There are so many theoretical subatomic particles that need to exist to make the math right. We haven't totally seen them yet, but we strongly suspect they exist. That's the beauty of math! Math is pure and it never lies. If the equation balances, then it points to the truth as best we know it, even if we can't produce a quantifiable, physically repeatable experiment. Sounds like God to me.

Unfortunately, the ideas and language of this world are not conducive to accurately expressing the meaning of such experiences. When we try to express our unique subjective perspective on the way we experience the ineffable episodes of living in the moment, we blurt out our experience with God and everyone immediately retrieves their personal version of God and dismisses the whole thing as some silly daydream.

We all crave love. We know it's real. Nobody has to prove to us that love is real, but where do you get it? Where does it come from? If everybody wants it and needs it so bad, why isn't there more of the stuff? Why is everyone on the planet starving for love? Mostly we don't know where to find it. We look for it everywhere in everyone we meet, but don't see it. The bible says, *"God is love"* and if that's true, then love is everywhere, and could possibly exist even inside you and me.

A Course in Miracles says: *"Nothing real can be threatened. Nothing unreal exists. Herein lies the peace of God."* If this is true then everything else is not real. We are in love. We are the creative conduits whereby God and love come into the world. Love flows through us to everyone around us if we let it, if we get ourselves out of the way, if we let go of our craziness and judgments. When we do this and the love flows, we are connected to all that is and experience a sense of divine affirmation as we witness his love through us to the world around us.

Wonderment & Awe

"The unexamined life is not worth living."-Socrates

One of my favorite books in college was an anthology of philosophical writings called, *"The Search for Meaning in Life."* It struck me as funny that my college taught a class about the meaning of life. I hadn't actually thought about it that much. I just assumed that everyone knew the meaning of life on some level. And then when I did think about it, I thought I already knew the answer. I guess everybody has worked out their own version of "the meaning of life." We don't much talk about it as we just do things and leave the reflections to anyone's that's interested in that sort of thing.

The question, "Who are you?" is usually answered by stating what you do and what you have and the things that interest you. It doesn't really answer the question, but we mostly don't probe beyond that initial answer. The Baby Boomers separate the winners from the losers based on how well we manage our busy schedules and by how much stuff we've collected. Our generation coined the phrase, "The person with the most toys at the end, wins." As a baby boomer, I assume we are all part of the gifted generation, the people that know everything there is to know by the sheer virtue of when we all arrived on the planet. (We all knew in the sixties that we already knew everything we needed to know!)

I look at the Generation Xers and the Millennium Generation and realize that every fresh generation believes and knows they are the gifted ones. One piece of common social knowledge then is the assumption that we all think we are the smartest humans that ever lived. We not only believe we know what we know, we believe we understand what we don't know and speak about it with great clarity.

You can't really begin to understand the meaning of life without a little self-examination. In the eastern religions there is a common metaphor for self-examination: They say self-discovery is like peeling an onion, one layer at a time. When you get to the end of the layers, you get to the heart of who you are. The truth is, when you get to the end of the layers, the center is empty! It's a magical, mystical existential riddle.

When we dig down through all the layers of cultural values, social values, and family values and then peel away all the thoughts, hopes, and ideas we've had about ourselves, we again end up with pretty much nothing. Well, not really nothing. What we find is a brand new life. We start with a baby, a blank slate, a tableau rasa. We travel back in time to that place where we were just beginning. What does it mean? Who am I? Who was I then and who am I now? How have I changed? We all ask ourselves these questions and wonder who we really are. Maybe a more telling question is, "Who do we think we are?"

Most of us struggle to discover who we are, or, we're covering up who we really are while pretending to be the person we think we need to be. Maybe we don't know anymore. Maybe we don't remember who we are. Maybe we got lost in this world and trying to find ourselves is more like an archeological excavation sifting through the emotional ruins of a lifetime of pretense.

It's very possible we've become a partially successful version of what Mom & Dad wanted us to be. We could actually be complete failures of what we thought our parents wanted us to be and living in the guilt of that disappointment, hiding out so to speak. For most of us, the real crime is the loss of our authentic self that was traded for a more practical version of who we thought we could be or needed to be.

Our parents weren't psychologists who understood the nature versus nurture equation in such a precise way they could have concocted the formula for our authentic selves. They did the best they could at the time. I love both my parents and know they did the best they could with me. You don't have to look any farther than the experience you've had with your own children when they decide it's going to be their way. Right then and right there we will lay down the law and teach them who's in charge. Do that enough times and pretty soon the baby learns to go underground and becomes "our good little baby". The Enneagram tells us there are nine distinct personality types, which are nine different ways we chose to survive infancy and childhood. They are the nine different ways we could behave to get our parent's attention to get what we needed to survive. It's actually a very accurate map of our personal characteristics. I'm a "two".

The Enneagram develops personality profiles that offer some insight into the relationship between the head and the heart. My chief feature as a two is: flattery. My higher mind is: will (freedom). My heart passion is: pride. My virtue is: humility. I am socially ambitious and a "me-first" kind of guy. Not surprising to me, a two is always looking for their real self because we have a hard time deciding who we really are. While a two can be very flattering, we are also capable of expressing unconditional love. It's very easy to figure out your own number even if you don't take the test. After reading about the characteristics of each number, you will be the number that you like the least.

I'm learning that God intends for us to see Him clearly as a Person. God is not an archetype or a good idea or bad idea as some people think. He is a Person. As the Apostle Paul says, *"We see dimly now, but later face to face."* Yet there are times we get a glimpse of His Divine Handiwork, a snapshot of eternity and see the role we are meant to play.

In these times, we experience in a clear way the immense size and beauty and mystery of our world and the universe itself. It is a moment that consumes us with wonderment and awe and in that solitary moment we seem to understand everything and take our place as part of all that is elegant perfection. It is this breath and vision we were born to behold, to be part of, and to live in. God is always with us and we believe He's busy somewhere else doing God things. We resist the idea that we are "what" He is doing. Somehow we just can't believe we are worthy of His attention. *We are what He is doing! He is very busy with us right now!*

The journey back to God is our journey and we make it as long and treacherous as we need it to be. It is measured only by the time of our foolishness and disbelief. When we get to the end of ourselves, God is there as He always has been, waiting for us to come home. It is a moment of wonderment and awe as we allow ourselves to be reconnected to Him. That is how it must be in heaven all the time. It can't be otherwise. Why did this take so long to happen to me?

I use the terms God and Jesus to describe the Ultimate Reality, the Creative Force of the Universe. That is my path and the way my heart, soul, and brain work together to understand the meaning of things. If you have a background in a different religious tradition, you can simply substitute whatever you choose for God and Jesus.

People are such skeptics about God. He isn't real! He's a device created by pathetic men to keep us in line to scare us into being good. God is blah! Blah! Blah! Whatever! When the new baby comes, and you look into the baby's face with wonderment and awe, you see God staring back at you and He looks much different than you thought He would. In that moment a bond is created with the child and the mother and father. It is an eternal bond, a bond of substance of two people coming together and creating a new being for the world. It is recognizing the expression of the combined DNA of two people creating a third person, a unique being; a new baby. (This event has never happened before in time unless you consider that it may have also actually happened in another universe, which we all know must exist, but can't prove.) It is the whole family and tribe coming together and closing together to form a ring of protection for the new life among us.

God certainly is in the middle of this ring right along with the baby. He is there with the baby and with us as we are all His forever. We each have our own path to the Divine, ultimate reality, and the infinite. Unfortunately, the history of the world is a history that does not practice religious tolerance or even tolerance for no religion at all. It should! We all need to learn to be more tolerant of a person's belief system. I'm learning that God does not need to be defended and or justified. He is! If some people don't see or believe, it's okay with me. They have not yet come to their time of understanding. This time of understanding comes to us all sooner or later.

When I stop and think about what I believe to be true, there is one overwhelming thing that I can't escape or dismiss: how much God respects us. Whether we believe in a personal God, an impersonal God, or no God at all, one thing we need to learn is, to respect everyone's personal beliefs. If it is true that God gave us free will, and many of us believe this to be true, then we can safely conclude that free will in a human being is something to be valued, even if we choose the wrong things.

If people don't believe the way we do, or believe in nothing at all, we faithful followers of whoever need to recognize a person's right to their own beliefs. After all, we Christians, believing we have received the truth, will mostly ignore it. We struggle to get it right. Sometime we do and sometimes we don't.

I'm always pleasantly surprised when I experience wonderment and awe. This state should be part of my daily life and yet, it doesn't happen as much as I'd like it to. How did I ever take my eyes off of this before? Why would I? Why do I just flip the switch and walk away from the peace that passes understanding and trade it in for all my worries and problems? My ego yanks on the choker chain and snaps me out of myself and back into my role. It's hard to take my toys to heaven with me. They don't seem important or necessary there. When I'm caught up in moments of wonderment my stuff is not that important. And when I try to bring heaven back to my every day, it just dissolves into a silly notion compared to the linear starkness of living in this world.

I guess the question is: How do we share our spiritual experiences? For us Christians, how do we become the true ambassadors of Christ? It's really the central question of our faith. If we can't believe it and live it, and become it, who will listen to what we have to say about it? Christ calls us to become the physical embodiment of his love. When we fail to become this love, which is often, we are back at square one. This is the present I'm always trying to unwrap. It's an ever-changing paradoxical puzzle and just when I seem to fit a few pieces together, the next piece doesn't fit at all.

In a solitary moment when I connect with someone else, I am back in His presence. It's not the big, big things. It's the small, small things that focus us on our work and bring us into His presence. Sometimes it's a glance, a hug, a quick conversation. Sometimes it's just being there with someone, and then it happens. It is as simple as staring into the eyes of a stranger and connecting with their soul and knowing them in a way that God intended for us to know each other all along. I may never see them again in this lifetime, and that's okay, because for an instant, we were connected, and the connection sparked an energy that propelled us both forward. I get connected and then I am connected back with Him and eternity and heaven and everyone I love. I am at oneness! I am! It is this communion that God intended for us all to share.

I've had this theory about the revolving door of life that happens on our planet. The Earth is a cosmic ride we're on for a short while. In the vastness of our ever-expanding universe, we know this one place as our home. If we're lucky, we get 80 good years to figure it all out. Then we die. We get a leg up as we read the recorded history of the world of other countries, cultures, and times. This history is the truth as we know it. The events may not have happened at all, but they are all part of the written record, part of our historic tradition. We spend time and energy to corroborate the facts, make little changes for accuracy, and then we buy it for ourselves.

I suspect every generation that ever lived, believed they were the chosen generation. Such are the fanciful ideas of our youth. We assume that everyone living before us was somehow less knowledgeable than we are now. Without study, without effort, we simply know we are better informed, better educated, and better equipped to move the world and all humanity forward into a better life.

It is an interesting dynamic that people come into the world at different times, in different cultures, and different families. The minute we arrive, the social compass starts recording magnetic north for us as we orient to our culture, the family, the city, the nation, and the time in our history. We are anchored in a specific social and cultural position on planet earth, our entry point of reference. Geologists examine the iron content in rocks, and from their alignment within the rocks, they can determine where magnetic north was when the rocks were formed. In some similar way, souls arrive on planet earth and are assimilated into the human family and oriented by virtue of family structure, culture, and date in history. The thread of our life is woven into the tapestry of civilization from that perspective. We are positioned in time and culture to develop and mature into that specific uniqueness which we already are. Each of us is an unknown variable with limitless possibilities of expressing what's inside us. We just need time to allow the seed of who we are to bloom into the full expression of our true form.

Maybe there is something more in the universe besides what our libraries can explain. Maybe the universe itself holds in-formation we don't fully understand. For example, there are about three dozen physical parameters of the universe that are required to be in perfect balance to allow the conditions for life to exist. Those parameters can be calculated and the odds of them all happening are astronomical. There is evidence that suggest that matter itself has some form of in-formation or intelligence to act the way it does. Why is the force of gravity stronger in the universe than the known mass suggests?

If the Big Bang was, in fact, a big explosion, how can there be such a harmonic ratio of everything throughout the universe? How do we interpret the values of such exquisite balance throughout the entire universe? Why do the smallest bits of physical matter not act the way we expect them to? They should always act the same, yet they seem to "know" what to do. These smallest bits of physical matter actually represent what we refer to as "reality." When we don't understand them, what can we then say about our understanding of reality? The question remains open for discussion.

One of the problems many of us face today is that we seem to have lost our sense of mystery about life. It may be a common assumption in our society today that we have reached the point in human history and in our lives where we understand everything about everything, or we almost do. And almost is close enough. We believe everything in the universe is somehow almost under our control and understood enough to be properly valued. We understand the sun and moon and all the stars. In our most arrogant self-delusion we believe we have become the masters of the universe and everything we say and do is the truth and meant to be so. This is an illusion. There is very little in the universe we can actually control. Given the enormous scale of nature mankind is not more than a little ant on the beach. Compared to the power of earthquakes, tsunamis, hurricanes, volcanoes, and asteroids, what we do is not very powerful at all.

The truth is each one of us is a unique key to the entire universe. We are the true mysteries to ourselves, and we don't bother to do the internal homework Socrates asked us to do. We should be studying ourselves, but that would be too painful. There's too much personal history, too much stuff we'd rather forget. There has never been anyone like us or even close to us. We are each our own galaxy. There is that much separation between us and everyone else as vast as the distances of space between galaxies. Do we ever really know another person? There is about as much chance of that as traveling to another galaxy. Do the math. But there is a way…..

Science has theorized wormholes-those anomalies of nature that allow travel through space without regard to time. Our scientists tell us that it is possible to overcome the extreme distances in space by traveling through wormholes. These anomalies somehow suspend the laws of the physical universe and allow miraculous travel to happen. The natural spiritual wormholes of our common humanity may be our hearts. Just as we will one day travel to distant galaxies through wormholes, we can now instantly connect with other people through our hearts. It's the main way to make the real power connection. It's may be the pathway God chose to reveal Himself to us. The human heart may be His wormhole He chose to create the connection to Him.

The problem is, we get our hearts broken at an early age and it closes up and doesn't work right and then we flush most of the rest of our lives down the toilet trying to be somebody else! This is the individual struggle to escape the gravitational pull of our family, social, and cultural orientation. We must also respect and consider our DNA as the genetic code that predetermines potentialities and defines limits to who we are. Our story is not much different than the salmon's struggle up river after so many years at sea. It is the way of nature for the strong to swim upstream against the current and to break through to the divine perspective of life. Not everyone gets there, but we must all try.

It is not the clever or brilliant or arrogant who get to that place of simple understanding and sublime peace. In His brilliance, God has made it so only the broken and defeated, the lowly and humble that are able to see clearly, to ascend to the divine view. There is a quality of present mental clarity that occur the instant you witness your complete brokenness. It dawns as a stark awareness at the edge of the known universe in your mind and then you understand how small you really are. It is the birth of gratitude and acceptance of the unknown and the unknowable. We must become completely empty vessels in order to contain the divine.

The waters of our soul need to be perfectly still to reflect the brilliant secrets that have been hidden from us. It is a different type of seeing. It is seeing without purpose, witnessing for the sake of being there to witness it. We cannot move a muscle without disturbing the vision. We can do little except witness the absolute perfection of everything God has created. Only in this meditative state, only in the moment of complete hopelessness, nothingness, only in this instant of being is it possible to see clearly enough to understand the message.

God has created all of this for us to find ourselves, to realize the perfection of His handiwork in us and for us to reflect back His glorious brilliance. In that moment, He lights us up with His presence and glorifies us and we reflect His light in the darkness. He only asks that we allow His light to shine in us and light the way for all our brothers and sisters that walk in darkness in the world. He asks our permission to love us. This is when we are each called to be the light bearers of truth in the world. Lao Tzu said, *"By letting it go it all gets done. The world is won by those who let it go. But when you try and try, the world is beyond winning."*

In the end, we find the path to enlightenment and self-awareness as a path of humility and service to others. It is accepting that we are all students of life and every single day is a new adventure for living. We need each other so much more than we realize. Who we are and what we do with our life is interdependent on everyone else. We simply aren't aware enough to see all the intricate connections and what they mean. Every single life is priceless. Every moment of every day in every life is a piece of the puzzle. It takes all seven billion of us working together in real time to solve the puzzle. WOW! The main thing we all need to do is to get on the same wavelength and that can be communicated. It can be transmitted. It can be understood. It's "The Butterfly Effect". Every little thing we do or don't do has an effect on everyone else in the world. We are all interconnected in such a way that what each of us does has an effect on all the rest of us. Put another way, if I can access what's going on with me, I can understand what's going on with everyone else. This is a manifestation of the collective unconscious and creates a unique dynamic in helping us focus where we are at in the present moment. You can do this as well as I can.

World peace relies on the idea that all the earth's resources can be marshaled in real time to serve the needs of the entire planet. This requires people to understand the socio-economic demands for every economy on earth in real time and to understand the manufacturing requirements of every segment of each economy. This must be executed in such a way that every social stratum in every economy is considered prior to the commitment of the resources. The next step involves a logistics solution to actually deliver the raw materials to the right place at the right time to keep the means of production efficient and to coordinate the necessary goods and services to flow where they are needed the most in real time. But before any of this can really happen, the citizens of the world need to agree to collaborate, to work together to create such a system.

In order for such a system to ever work, we all need to learn to believe in each other. We must trust each other and this can never happen until we can all experience a level of tolerance, understanding, and compassion or what I call, wonderment and awe, for all human life no matter the social, political, religious, or ethnic origin. We are all related. We are all one. This will never happen until we achieve a common bandwidth, a shared coherence, or as some say, we all start vibrating at the same frequency.

Buddha said, *"If you do not tend one another, then who is there to tend you? Whoever would tend me, he should tend the sick."* It's a simple lesson, but one that falls on deaf ears in our modern world. There is no commercial value in helping the marginalized people in our world. They can't buy anything, so they don't matter. As long as we are not doing everything in our power to help each other we will remain spiritually marginalized ourselves and no amount of preaching makes a difference. We Christians are called to value what the rest of the world considers worthless. Until the blessed minority steps down from our pulpits and pedestals and embrace the life struggles going on all around us, we can't even start the journey home. We all go together or we don't go at all!

And there are many, many churches walking the talk today and reaching out to those who need help and effectively nourishing and nurturing people's bodies and souls. They just don't show that stuff on the evening news. It is not newsworthy! Most of us can manage a small project, a single person, or maybe two people. It is not the size or the cost of the gift, but the heart of the giver. These small acts of charity are opportunities to extend wonderment and awe in our world.

Hypocrites, Liars, & Cowards

"All that we are is the result of what we have thought. If a man speaks or acts with an evil thought, pain follows him. If a man speaks or acts with a pure thought, happiness follows him, like a shadow that never leaves him."-
The Buddha

The devil comes to visit me every night around 3:00 AM, opens my head, and claws at my brain. I can do nothing but pray and hope he goes away soon. I am not more than one course at the buffet for him. In the dark he accuses me of being a liar and a hypocrite and not worthy of God's love. He plays on my emotions and tells me, "God could never love you! He says He does, but, take a good look at yourself! How could He? You are a liar! You lie to yourself and you lie to God. And He knows it! You think you're forgiven because of Jesus? Ha! You're only fooling yourself. You don't really believe God loves you because you know He doesn't. He doesn't love you because you are unlovable." Then he leaves. He just vanishes in the night air. He leaves me alone in the dark to ponder his words...to refute them...to embrace them...to reject them...to mull them over for some level of substance...for a grain of truth.

So begins the nightly accounting of my soul, weighing it against what I believe, against my experience, against what? It requires me to run through all the situations of my life and to render a verdict. Guilty! Guilty! I am a harsh judge, and so I spend the rest of my night in prayer asking for forgiveness, begging for it, and hoping someone is listening. I can't sleep as I feel my blood burning my body from the inside out. After he leaves, my mind gets busy wandering through my past and I don't wander very far before I find volumes of books, and each book tells a story of how I've failed, disappointed, hurt, blamed, shamed, hid, lied, and run away from myself and everyone I love. I had no opinions, no thoughts, no feelings, only drifting through each day to get by somehow…..to not bruise or offend…to not hurt those around me. I remember all the stupid terrible things I did, not out of meanness, only selfish ignorance, but that's enough to convict me. Such are the meals we prepare for ourselves and others when we abdicate our freedoms and allow our emotions full expression or choose to stay quietly uninvolved.

I am "the good Christian" that doesn't get involved because "it's not my business". I confess I am a hypocrite, liar, and coward, but not always and not in every situation. Sometimes I'm capable of doing the right thing, of understanding, showing compassion, tenderness, even love, but it's only by grace, by God's love that I'm able to do any of it. Sometimes I will even take a stand and declare my position, but mostly I don't. Sometimes I help the poor or offer an encouraging word, but mostly I don't. Sometimes my head comes out of the self-absorbed fog and sees the plight of others less fortunate than myself, but mostly it doesn't.

The world now is ablaze with every hell known to man. The twenty-first century presents challenges we have never experienced before in history. It is the largest stage ever constructed where we can be present in every corner of the world at the same time and eavesdrop on even the smallest human calamities everywhere at once. We are now hooked on a daily, hourly, and real time dose of tragedy, calamity, and human misfortune. Human misery is beamed into every TV set and Internet site around the world in real time, all the time. "We interrupt our regular programming to bring you this breaking news…breaking news happens every hour now on TV."

How can we endure the weight of such continuous misfortune? How can we see this and hear this news every day and not go numb? What can I do? What can we do? The news leaves us stunned and powerless for a while and then indifference sets in as a safeguard against the onslaught of the horrific. We learn to adjust our sensitivities to the severity of the news and dose ourselves to an acceptable level of human pain and deeper levels of emotional numbness. We just blink out and the lights go dim. We float downstream, lifeless, toward the sea of sorrow becoming human debris with little hope we can ever change the outcome of anything anywhere in our world.

Our new society has created the perfect social cocktail of affluence, notoriety, and easy access to fame via the Internet, YouTube, Facebook, and Twitter. The current expectation is that we should have it all. We believe blindly that our social reality and governments will somehow save us, protect us, and provide for us. The social fabric of today is strongly intertwined with all things economic, so everything is for sale. We are no longer people and citizens, but commodities to be managed from cradle to grave for profit. It is impossible to ignore someone's apparent social status and we rarely bother with basic human needs. People either have medical insurance or they don't. They either have jobs or they don't. It is so easy to join the army of marginalized citizens nowadays. Many of us are not more than a couple of paychecks from the street. Missed opportunities, lack of benevolent benefactors, starting the race after everyone else only to find you've been running in the wrong direction the whole time are all factors in the great game of life. Churches and religious institutions try to fill the gap. Even the prosperous churches, the wealthy congregations, the powerful elite members of the blessed kingdom offer some measure of grace to the unfortunate. The poorer churches are barely able to keep their doors open. Others do more harm than good. God bless them all. We Christians realize the guilt in our hearts and confess our sins, but we must do much more. We must be willing to give it all up and follow Christ into the streets, into the darkness of humanity, and do what we can.

It's common knowledge that the church is filled with hypocrites, liars, and cowards. As Christians, we would all stand up and say, "Yea, that's about right", knowing our own hearts and confessing our failures before God and everyone else. From the outside looking in, the world seems to have the opinion that the Christian church thinks it enjoys some level of moral superiority above all other forms of religion. The church is judged by the actions of a few and the deeds of the many go unnoticed and unacknowledged. Many people in the world believe the Christian faith is not much more than the self-delusion of Christmas on earth and pie in the sky-that being a Christian is a way to get the things you want in this world. There are others who don't know a thing about theology, but gratefully accept the food, clothing, and medicine provided by the many global church humanitarian projects.

Christians are labeled as narrow-minded pompous idiots that go around blathering this doctrine or that doctrine without substance, without reason or concern for their fellow man or woman and for no other reason than to make themselves feel good. I'm sure there are times when we all act this way whether we are Christian, Jew, Hindu, Buddhist, Atheist, Agnostic or even Jedi Knight. The examples of some do not condemn the many. Everyone should have the right to their own beliefs! There are millions of believers that do nothing more than quietly serve the needs of others without ever thinking of anything more than helping someone and being useful. Many of these blessed givers are poor people themselves, but recognize a greater need in others, and actually do something about it!

The truth is all religious systems offer some kind of definition for who we are in the cosmos. There may be some among us who need no definition at all to know who they are. Here in the United States our citizens enjoy the freedom to follow any religion they choose without fear of reprisal, attack, or condemnation, and this includes atheists, many of whom believe they are persecuted! This is far from the truth as we read about the banning of public prayer in schools and sporting events, and the elimination of teaching any creation theory in schools. It seems that atheists are in vogue at the moment and it appears unfashionable to believe in anything religious at all.

There are many of us that believe evolution and creation theories do not need to be mutually exclusive. Beyond the ideas of biological evolution are other ideas such as the thoughts regarding the Akashic Record of the universe and the concept that the universe itself has a form of intelligence. There are also many cosmological questions that must be answered before we can render a verdict on this topic, which greatly broadens the scientific scope of any investigation. And while these topics are interesting and relevant as social topics, we will do well to at least respect everyone's personal belief system with some level of toleration. My expressions of faith happen to be Christian. That's how I understand the ultimate realty of things. I could even be completely wrong about all of it, but it is my belief system!

The effective Christian church on earth has only one mission: to preach the Good News and this is best done with some food, clothing, shelter, medicine, and money to help those in need. The church on earth is to be found nowhere at all and everywhere at once. It is comprised of the hearts and minds and spirits of those pathetic souls who have exhausted themselves and got to the end and given up the ghost. God is the last choice we have, the last stop on our own personal magical mystery tour we've crafted for ourselves. Only the hopeless will take the time to search their souls for the meaning of their suffering and in so doing, find God waiting for them. The rest of us play at our religion like homework we must do to earn a passing grade. The church on earth is everywhere and so are liars, hypocrites, and cowards.

On our faith journey, every Christian comes to understand the depth of our own hypocrisy and cowardice. We learn that the truth is not in us. Christians realize they are beggars to the cross as Martin Luther stated. As beggars to the cross, we have no right to exclude anyone else from being there with us. We have no elevated social station except to be the foot-washers and helpers of everyone else. The general population of the unchurched looks upon the church without knowing our heart and without understanding what we believe. All I would ever ask is for people to examine the evidence, visit a church, read the bible for yourself, and search your heart. The answers will come.

We Christians know that we cannot please God by what we do. We can't earn it ourselves. There is no moral superiority among us. The only distinction between Christians and non-Christians is that Christians claim to understand God's grace and have pledged to share the same grace with anyone who will have it. As a Christian it's clear enough to me to acknowledge my sins before God and before every man as well. I am a sinner! I have not chosen God, but He chooses me and reveals himself to me in a million ways. It doesn't matter what direction I look; He is there. Even when I've denied Him, He is still there!

I've finally learned that God is so real it would be crazy to continue to deny Him and His wisdom is made all the clearer when I finally bring myself to see the insanity of human action in the world I live in. We Christians have no cloak of respectability to wrap ourselves in. We cannot claim any level of moral superiority. We are no better except we believe we are loved. We have embraced "The Good News". We have accepted God's gift gratefully. That's the only difference.

If non-believers can't embrace the notion of God's grace for us, maybe we can at least recognize a feeble willingness to fully embrace our humanity with an open mind and open heart that is, a non-judgmental heart and mind. When we do this, we are left with only one question: What will I do to help? What can I do to help others? We are left with a simple understanding of ourselves and the human condition. Feed me! Clothe me! Give me shelter! Comfort me and give me warmth! Help me to understand who I am in the world! The God of the universe asks us to honor His children no matter what is in their heart or mind, believer or unbeliever alike.

I am a confessed hypocrite, liar, and coward, but I continue to believe in the goodness of God, in the salvation of God through His Son, Jesus of Nazareth, and in the wisdom of the bible. I finally get it. It took a lot of years, but it all makes sense to me now. I no longer have the time in my life to wait around until I think I'm good enough for God. I never will be! After my mom died and then my aunt died and then my brother died, I got it. I am finally beginning to understand. I loved them so much and I realize now that until someone dies, I never really knew how much of my heart they occupied and then I knew for sure. My heart is hollowed out like a bowl of guacamole. It's empty! I know how silly I was to have wasted so much time on stupid selfish things and not spending the time loving them and just being with them. For all of us, someday, we learn how precious life is, that true wealth is never valued in money, but in time and time spent loving the people around you, sharing yourself and your heart with them.

And then….then and only then do we begin to calculate and respect the value of love and what it is and what it means…and then, slowly it breaks you down, breaks down your illusions, and even more slowly you begin to understand the way the world turns and rotates, the way it revolves around the sun and the way the sun spins in its own orbit in the solar system, and its relationship to the galaxy…and then, it dawns on me that I didn't know much about anything. I was wrong about everything. I'm still learning since life and living in the moment have my full attention now.

Living in the Kingdom of NOW

"There is a moment between the breath going in and the breath going out that we are not breathing at all. In that small moment of NOW, it is possible to see everything clearly."-Richard Smith

I remember sitting with my Great Grandpa on his front porch, watching the sun go down, and feeling the heat radiating from the concrete. The moment right after sunset was the very best. The warm air hung there all around us without moving, as the day quietly faded away with the sunlight. Few words were said as we sat, night after night, watching the day end together. Life was simply passing time with my Grandpa. I didn't need to know anything else. I knew then I was going to have a great life, but I didn't know that I didn't need to know anything else.

My earliest memories are of my great grandpa and grandma. My world is forever colored by passing time with them. Every day was a slow, leisurely meal. We got up and after a while, we had coffee and then breakfast. After breakfast, we strolled around outside, got out in the morning air for a while, and then settled in for a quiet morning. It wasn't long until it was lunchtime, or dinnertime as grandma called it. We took afternoon naps, talked a little, and then got ready for supper. The afternoons were the very best. We didn't turn on the TV, but sat there doing whatever we were doing. My whole being was absorbed in complete silence, except for the train whistle once in a while and the clock ticking in the kitchen.

My great grandparents didn't say more than ten words an hour, yet we were all connected in each passing moment, alone and yet together at the same time. It was a way of being I learned at an early age. It was wonderful to hear the train whistle in the distance and feel that sound fill up our consciousness as it broke the silence we'd been enjoying. I have lived in many different places in this town since those days, and I can still hear the train's whistle as I lay in bed at night. It connects me to sixty years of memories. The sound of the train in the distance always brings me back to those carefree days before school at grandpa and grandma's.

These were my earliest memories. From the moment we are born, our mind begins to develop a sense of who we are in the world (separation) and we grow accustom to being alone with our internal dialog. Whether we read out loud or silently to ourselves, we always say the words in our head. Who is the internal speaker? Each of us creates a separate reality in our head where all life's dramas are played out. We somehow develop the ability to compare our thoughts to others as we listen to what they are saying and as a way to benchmark our development, to make sure we are okay, to make sure we are connected. How do we ever know for sure? How do we ever really know someone else? How do we define the criteria and navigate the social skills for sharing experiences? There seem to be innate child skills that helped us take those first social steps, that helped us create a "we" from an "I."

Our attention shifts between the internal and the external and we notice ourselves being different from what we have known about ourselves. We develop social consciousness. The trick is how do we get out of our own little kingdom and live in the kingdom God invites us to enter? How do we become the people He made us to be instead of the person we created to survive the world around us? How do we even know there is another way? How can we keep our individual identity and yet be part of the coherent whole in the world?

I've learned to look for the answers to these questions in my heart. Even though the doing of the things in life seem to be generated and steered by thoughts in the mind, the meaning of life is experienced through feelings in the heart. It's confusing to us at such an early age, because the head and the heart seem to be the same thing, seem to be connected and working together. As we grow and move deeper into the world around us, our comfortable kingdom gives way to the greater reality of our place in a social structure. As members of a family, we settle into our role and our place in the family structure and the dynamic takes over. We conform and play the role.

When we leave the family we can choose to play another role, but it is still a role mostly defined by the emotions and values we learned in the family. This is when many of us wander off into the wilderness of pain without family, thinking, "I'm not going to do *that* anymore!" We will only ever reclaim our rightful position when we find our authentic self, the person we are meant to be. The kingdom of now is not won with theological arguments, human morality, or church dogma. It is found in the simple wisdom of our heart that we knew so long ago in our childhood. The Buddha says, *"Peace comes from within. Do not seek it without."*

It is not possible for God to ever stop loving us. It is entirely possible that we can ignore this gift without a second thought. After all, God speaks to our hearts in such a small voice, we rarely listen to Him. It may now be time for us to pause from our busy schedules and take inventory of the contents of our heart. If we do this now, we can begin to sift through the rubble, get rid of the junk and set aside all we hold dear to us. That inventory is all that ever matters, now and in all eternity. Take a breath. Take a moment. Take an hour. Take a day. Take the rest of your life to slowly release the beautiful gift of yourself to everyone in your world. *You are God's* message to me and to everyone else. He has wrapped His brilliance and love and grace and beauty in your smile, in the softness in your voice, in your eyes, and in your presence. You *are his beloved!* We find this hard to believe about ourselves.

The brilliance of heaven is hidden among the imagined ruins of doubt, fear, and a general sense of loss. We've learned to recognize our weaknesses and liabilities and taken steps to keep those things hidden from view long ago. We don't want people seeing them, yet these are the things God uses to work His will in the world. He meets us exactly at our most broken point, a place where we cannot take another step, another blow, another fall. We know we won't get up the next time. In these moments we need to take a deep breath and find our self between the inhale and the exhale. And there we are. Your beauty is ageless. It is without time. It is eternal.

In God's Kingdom, He has given His children hearts to see that which is ageless. He calls us to be children, and when we do, we remember the dazzling mystery of life as we once knew it. We rediscover ourselves in the eyes of others. We cultivate the ability to see the little boy or little girl we hid away so long ago. We can do this when we are in communion with each other. That is who we truly are living in the Kingdom of NOW. It is not a faraway place. Heaven (or the Kingdom of NOW) is right HERE, right NOW. It is inside me, you, and everyone. We're lost in our head and we'll never ever find it there because the kingdom of NOW and the Kingdom of heaven do not exist in our head. It exists in our heart. We let it go long ago when we traded it for "something better" as we struggled to become who we thought we (wanted) to be. But how do we get it back? How do we find our way back home?

Somehow it seems natural to look for the answer outside of our self, to expect someone to rescue us, to save us. We trust the objective finding of external observations and quantified conclusions of our science experiments. We have unshakable faith in our mathematical equations and cosmological theories. The modern mind is squarely entrenched in the illumination of Darwin's Theory and we seem to know almost everything for sure. This information explains a great deal about the physical universe around us, but does little to help us understand who we are in the cosmos.

The last place we want to look is deep into our own hearts. We don't want to look into the mirror for fear of what we will see. We are comfortable with the slightly adorable compulsive monster that stares back at us or the almost important someone that didn't get the lucky break, but should have. It doesn't matter what image we see in the mirror. The message is the same, "It's not my fault. I'm off the hook. I just want to slide by in this life and pretend I could have been somebody important." And with that we create all the excuses we ever need to never face another issue. We accept that we are "good enough" and not responsible. We avoid the cosmic accountability of life to life of life for life. We've answered the question and believe we are not our brother's keeper. We miss the truth of our own importance and the connection to each other.

We fabricate a cosmology for our personal reality that seems to strike a balance for us. In this delusion we craft scenes that appear granite-like, which in fact, have the substance of cotton candy. It all seems so real! We want to believe it is real as we've bet everything on the picture. Our identity is anchored in the trick, the sleight of hand of the mind. Where is the substance? Where is the basis in fact? We assume our minds are steel traps and we can't be fooled. We embrace the magical daydream, and toss the real version in the waste basket. We believe our tender age is sufficient time to have generated an accurate historical perspective- our basis in reality. We buy the lie hook, line, and sinker. How many people have lived for 1000 years? How about a million? How about a billion? We each get about 80 years. That's nothing in geological time!

For many of us, 80 years seems too long considering all the frustrations and power failures we experience. When I finally got on the path and actually started doing the work of the soul, life itself became unbearable. Everything became a frustration. The simplest things created difficulties and presented insurmountable challenges for me. It was as if Life itself conspired against me, against my decision to seek wholeness. It was as if Life wanted me to struggle and work for it. Once I crossed over to the other side, I couldn't go back. Every simple task became a cacophonous blast of uninterested sound in my symphony of goals. I could no longer fabricate illusions to make me feel better.

The truth has a way of burning all the bridges to the past and I was left alone with the present moment, to ponder, to wonder, to embrace it and live in it. I have become aware that I'm aware and that can't be undone without serious consequences. It's at this point I began to understand the depth of my poverty, my cowardice, my utter failure as a creature. It is at this exact moment in the process of awakening that grace becomes an option. I became aware of a way out of this mess I'd created. This fork in the road allowed me a path to redemption, to salvation, to wholeness. It was a spiritual awakening and a moment of awe. The Buddha said, *"Do not dwell in the past; do not dream of the future, concentrate the mind on the present moment."*

The best we can ever do is simply marvel at the handiwork, live in the moment, embrace the mystery, and be grateful for the experience. It's as if we are all walking around in a dark cave feeling our way for the light switch. We are not so much afraid of being unimportant. That's what we want. We're terrified that we are something more, something much more. None of us wants to be "the one" and we each are the one because we are each unique and necessary. We prefer the darkness of the cave rather than rediscovering our true selves. It frightens us that so many people depend on us. We don't want the responsibility.

As I go deeper and deeper into the cave, I'm seeing the brilliance that God put inside me and it's frightening! I have no more excuses other than I'm bashful, I'm shy, I might be wrong, I'm small….no I'm a coward. I'm afraid to step out there in the real world and let everyone see who I really am. I'm afraid people won't like me and I'm afraid they will.

Jesus said, *"If anyone thirsts, let him come to me and drink. He who believes in me as the scripture has said, "Out of his heart shall flow rivers of living water."* John 7:37-38. This is the work we are all called to do. You'll know (you've arrived) when love starts flowing out of you like living water. I find meditation helps me to peel away the layers of illusion of what I think I am. It allows my heart and soul to open up, to blossom into fullness, just in the moment, just for now. The human heart cannot contain the love of the universe when we are in alignment with it. It gushes right out of us and we can't sit still. We can't stay quiet. We have to speak! We have to act! We have to be!

Living in the Kingdom of Now means we begin to let go of temporary things and embrace our true nature and our role in the eternal drama. It means opening the eyes of our heart to the brilliant light and love and power of heaven that is all around us and flowing through our hearts if we will only allow this to happen! Once the heart valve is open and the Spirit starts flowing, it will be a startling moment. The lights of the universe all come on and we stand in that bright light of illuminated understanding and being. When the flow stops, that is the exact moment we flip the "on switch" to our egos and try to harness the power of heaven for our own purpose. It doesn't work that way. We will have discovered the "on" and "off" switch to our power. The rest of our lives we struggle to keep the switch turned on while our ego works to flip the switch again and again to plunge us back into darkness and chaos.

We become aware that we are in charge of very little, yet with one step we can say "yes" to life, "yes" to ourselves, and "yes" to express our meaning and understanding. We are ultimately silent witnesses to the eternal process of creation. Our egos feverishly struggle to manufacture an artificial reality as quickly as it is needed. It has no substance! It produces only dead-end roads that lead to nowhere. The crazy part is we keep driving down those dead-end roads as if they were shortcuts to our own personal heaven. We always end up right back where we started, but we think, "one day my shortcut will pay off. One day I'll be right," and it never happens. It's never going to happen! In the moment of now we find our center and all the energy we ever need.

I'm living every day in this world of flesh and blood, taxes and death, worry and struggle, winning and losing. As far as I can tell, this is the human condition. This is my condition. Somehow in the thick of it, I'm learning to find shelter from the storm, to find the center of my being and hold on. I used to be caught up in the winds and blown all over. That still happens, but now I can slow down and focus on just being in the moment. Suddenly, that's enough! The storm is still there, but it's around me, not in me. I am not part of the fury. I am me and I can simply witness the chaos around me and choose not to participate in it. I have found refuge when I am completely still and realize I am totally dependent on God, completely engulfed in the stillness of Him. In that space I can breathe, I can be. The moment I get a taste of my own power I'm back in the chaos and struggle of the storm.

I've been satisfied with quick glimpses of paradise, moments of light and brilliance, a whiff of eternity, and then endless periods trekking through the valley of the shadow of death, slugging it out spiritually, dragging a knapsack of lifelong miseries. No matter how swiftly I ascend or how much elevation I grapple for, in an instant I snap back into the valley of the shadow of death and the prison cell of self-doubt. I'm back in the mental prison I crafted with my own guilt and shame.

I know there is a Zen place for each of us where we can put ourselves in neutral and exist in harmony of everything around us. It's like the entire universe is rotating around me and I am the very center of it all. There is such stillness, calm, and clarity in this place. When I get in this place, I never want to leave. I can see all eternity from my little perch, my little space here. I'm not bothering anyone and it feels like I actually belong here. The problem I always have is finding my way to this place. With all the business of life most of the time it's hard to believe this place exists anywhere except in a pipedream. It really exists!

Living in the Kingdom of Now is a gift given to me. It is not a future event. It exists in the present moment and all I need to do is reach out and grab it. All I have left is what is left of my life and it's all you have too. We can choose to continue on the hamster wheel we've been on all our life or step into the kingdom of the everlasting. It's a choice between sanity and insanity, between illusion or truth, between love and fear. At some point in our lives, we've taken all the punches we can absorb and decide to quit trading blows. When we finally get to the end of the fight, with nothing left inside, God is there, waiting as He always has been. He collects us up into His everlasting love and brings us to the place we were always meant to be. With every breath we take, we breathe in life, love, power, and purpose… the intentionality that God originally made for us. We find our authentic selves and discover we've been living in the kingdom all along. Silly me! I thought I was in charge of everything.

The WOW Factor

"Sooner or later we find ourselves in front of a door that beckons us to enter. It is our door, made only for us to use. We will open it and find out what's on the other side, or continue walking along the same familiar safe path, not knowing what we missed, or what direction our life may have taken"

-Richard R. Smith.

When I woke up on January 1st, 2010, I knew it was a different kind of New Year's Day. I knew I had to figure out something different for my life, or this could be my last year on earth. For many of us, January 1st is a sober day with most of us recovering from the celebration of the night before, ushering in the New Year and all of that stuff. For me, every January 1st is mostly a lost day. It's a non-holiday holiday. It's cold outside and there's not much to celebrate anyway. This January 1st was the first one after my heart attack and after spending eight months getting used to all the new drugs I had to take to keep me alive, I arrived at "the proverbial" fork in the road.

After eight months of being thankful to still be alive, adjusting to the new direction of my life, and it being January 1st and all, I had the whole day to ponder my situation. We only get so many laps around the track before we cross the finish line and this year seemed like it could be my last lap. Life is hard enough when you're young, beautiful, and healthy. I didn't have any of these things going for me. So I thought, "What can I do this year to keep myself going, to make a difference, to contribute? What is my new life all about?" That was the big question.

After a while, I realized there was something I could do. I decided to write a one-page article for my church newsletter every month for the whole year. It was a fairly meager task. I set the bar low for myself, but I had to. That's all I could do. I had no vision beyond that one little task. It felt good and I almost believed that God blessed it. I was able to draw a line in the sand. I understood that I could not retreat from this humble goal. It seemed it was all I had left to fight with. Little did I know that 2010 would contain events that would take my life in a direction I had not intended. I never see these things coming, and probably most people don't either. We look forward to a future where everything happens as we expect it should. It's somewhat predictable. The future we get is not the future we envision, and life takes us where we need to go, not necessarily where we want to go.

I arrived at the Radisson early, bought a coffee, and started searching for the "WOW Factor" conference room. I was hoping this whole thing would be worth it, would be something healthy for me. When I finally found the room, the door was open, but the room was empty. I went inside and waited. Shortly, people started drifting in and finally my friend Arsen showed up and then Lynn arrived. They start setting up for the event. I remember Lynn from the other event in March. Eventually everyone that signed up for this event arrived. There were nine of us, and as we settled in, I was growing more hopeful for an action-packed weekend of learning something new, and maybe gain some inside knowledge on how to become a better public speaker. My expectations at that moment in time were so one-dimensional. Before the weekend was over, I learned that knowledge is one-dimensional, experience is three dimensional, and unconditional love is multi- dimensional. All the people in the room seemed like normal people. As I studied each person in the room, my thought drifted to questions about who they were, why they were here, and how this whole thing would turn out.

It's difficult to describe what happened the rest of the weekend. Some people believe in fate, pre-destination, divine revelation, cause and effect, stream of consciousness, precognition, ESP, and yes, even miracles. Seven of these people were complete strangers to me. Arsen was a friend, but we didn't really hang out together. We'd known each other about five years, but I didn't get to know who he was until March when I attended his event at the Saroyan Theater in Fresno and met Lynn Rose. I didn't meet her as much as I watched her from the audience while she single-handedly managed the magical parade of the most brilliant people I had ever seen or heard in my life. Arsen's event in March connected me with exactly the people my heart needed to be connected to and made me realize there was hope for me. This guy that I had sort of known for five years brought together the most amazing, illuminating, and soulful people I'd ever seen together at the same time on the same stage. That day changed my life. Arsen's authentic presence gave me permission and hope that I might also have an authentic self.

We like to think we know ourselves pretty well. Most of us have spent a fair amount of time thinking about life, about who we are, who we think we are, and about why we're alive. What is our purpose in all of humanity? It's not a far reach from the truth to believe we think of ourselves as being smart and capable of learning, of knowing fact from fiction, of discerning the truth in all things. Our lifeline shows a steady increase in education, usable knowledge, career advancement, smart shopping, good choices, the right values, and at some point, we feel like we're standing on solid ground in our assessment of ourselves and where we're at in life. I know I was, but all that was about to change for me.

The WOW Factor is a two-day very intense workshop dedicated to helping people become effective public speakers, but it is also much more. I wasn't concerned about becoming a professional speaker or thinking about making money as a public speaker or making a career change. My two little goals for the weekend were very humble: My hope was to learn some speaking techniques that would help me become a better preacher and I hoped I could learn to be a more interesting and engaging teacher when I conducted training at work. That was it! My mind was open for the knowledge. I did have a third reason; I was hoping it would be fun enough to help kick me out of the nagging depression I'd been in for about six months. It just kept hanging on and dragging me down every single day and I thought if I could just get a little traction here this weekend, maybe I could climb out of the pit and be normal for a while.

When the class started, Lynn began explaining some of the things we'd be learning and Arsen was running the camera and popped in every now and then to share his enthusiasm for what was about to happen explaining this was his second WOW Factor. It got me excited because the only reason I was here was because of Arsen. He had attended a WOW Factor course the previous October and said it changed his life. And that's where this whole thing started because out of that event, Arsen produced his event in March at the Saroyan called, "The Time of Your Life is Now" which was one of the single best days of my entire life and a day that gave me hope that I could do something good with whatever life I had left. Back in March I was in month three of my depression, and when Arsen invited me to his event, I agreed to go. I was looking forward to it half-heartedly, but it was a day away from work and I decided it was going to be a day for me. On that day, I learned how awesome Arsen is! What I want to say (and what I'm ashamed to say) that, on the day I went to Arsen's event, I was struggling with finding reasons to keep on living. I'm not the suicide-type, but I was empty and had been drifting without meaning for months. My day at Arsen's show changed everything. Arsen, 75 years old, had quadruple bypass surgery a few years ago, and at 74, he reinvented himself! He is a joy and an inspiration to all of us and everyone that knows him. Arsen showed me that I was not a lost cause and in fact, maybe I actually had something to share, to give back to life.

Lynn Rose is an incredible force. She is an amazing singer, speaker, and human being. She is soulful, intelligent, and a brilliant presence! Her light shines brightly when she's doing her thing. It's hard to believe she is a real person. During our two days at the WOW Factor, there were many tears, laughs, and hugs. Lynn doesn't teach you as much as she plays with you and gives you permission to be a kid again. It's all part of the journey into the heart. Learning to speak from your heart and connecting with your audience is a byproduct of what happens to you during this process. The core accomplishment is the unexpected miracle of reconnecting to your authentic self. During this journey deep into the heart, there are tears of joy, tears of sorrow, and tears of gratitude. In some ways the work you do at WOW Factor is the most intimate human contact we may ever have with each other. It is pure, childlike, honest, and revolutionary. You go deep into your hearts and everyone's heart during the exercises, and, in the process experience a profound, miraculous transformation and a powerful connection with the group members.

In an instant, my consciousness, body, mind, spirit, soul, and heart disappeared, and I was simply a being. I was. I was there. In those transforming moments, I understood that everything in the world has a life and a purpose of its own. On some level, I knew that everything is connected, every situation unfolds for a purpose, and also, knowing that we are all supported by a divine being, no matter how bad things might seem. I felt I was in heaven, the real heaven, but still in the room. All the grief I had ever carried, all the worries, and fears just fell off me and were gone forever. I could feel the garbage my heart had so carefully collected over my lifetime lying there on the floor in a pile. Looking around the room at Lynn and my classmates, I knew that I had always known them. I can't explain exactly what happened in those moments of brilliant light. Maybe it was a vision, maybe madness, maybe standing in the Glory of God, or maybe it was a shining moment of cosmic consciousness. I don't know for sure. I know it was an experience that completely transformed me forever. There was no more time, no more separation, and no more pain. We are all connected! We are all forever connected and cannot be unconnected unless we accept our separation as the ultimate reality. Our egos demand we separate from everyone else and once we are alone, there is no defense. We're done! When this connection happened to me I instantly knew I somehow needed to find a way to stay connected. I want every single human being to have what I got in that moment!

You ask, "Exactly what happened to you? How can I have this experience too?" I guess my short answer would be to attend a WOW Factor event. This book is my attempt to explain what I experienced and what it has meant to me. Your experience will yield different and unique results and insights. Since then I've studied and reflected and come to understand that the exercises Lynn lead us through during the WOW Factor took us so quickly and deeply into our hearts that we didn't have time for our normal defense mechanisms to work. In an instant, Bam! You are right in the middle of your real self, face to face, and a little startled and dazed. There is a realization of something found, of something that had been lost, and you are reunited with who you really are, who you have always been, always knew that you knew this, and somehow fooled yourself into believing you were somebody else. I saw my beautiful self as I was intended to be. I can see that beauty in other people, but never believed I could be beautiful as well. It is the most profound and startling revelation a person can have in this world. I had it and will forever hold that vision! I now understand it better and want every single person on the planet to have it. The experience filled up my heart to overflowing to the point that I simply must share what I learned with everyone. If everyone doesn't experience this thing I went through, I know the world won't get any better. I know I can't get any better. We are all more deeply connected that we ever imagined.

What happened, what I remember experiencing, is that large bands of energy that I would describe as love, came gushing out of my heart and flowed directly into the hearts of everyone in the room. The communion and communication was natural and seemed to be the way we are meant to communicate with each other. I'm not sure what I was saying. It didn't seem to matter. The words didn't matter except they were the data packets we were sharing. We were sharing a moment in time and we were all solidly connected into one being.

In those moments I understood our potential as creatures and I'll say it this way- as God originally intended us to live. I also understood clearly how much He loves us. There is no condemnation of us from God. He loves all of us, even those of us who know we are unworthy and those that think they are worthy and atheists and the very religious among us! He loves the arrogant and the greedy as much as He loves the humble and down-trodden. He may be disappointed with our behavior but He loves us! I learned in that state of transformation that I had no desire for money, power, fame, or anything except an overwhelming urge that every single human being needs to experience this thing I'm going through. I believe we all will experience it sooner or later. I prefer sooner as it will help shorten the time and amount of human misery we all share together.

The experience of Lynn Rose's WOW Factor is an experience of Lynn herself. What you get for your money is the real thing, the thing you didn't look for, the thing that once you get you will never, ever let go of. Lynn's brilliance becomes evident as each step in the process unfolds and we learn the craft of public speaking from our hearts while we are going deeply into our hearts. She has a money-back guarantee, but nobody ever wants their money back. One of the most amazing things about the weekend experience is to witness how moving it is for Lynn. I'm sure each WOW Factor is a little different and unique and I cannot fathom how her heart manages the incredible volumes of love and closeness and intimate connections that occur during the training. If you attend a WOW Factor, your experience will be a unique journey into the very heart of life. For me, I had the luxury to bask in the afterglow with my local new found WOW Factor companions, while Lynn had to move on to her next assignment in her busy schedule. (She drove home at the end of our class and left Fresno at midnight and didn't get home until around 4:00AM)

It's been four months since my WOW Factor experience and every single day my mind is occupied with Lynn and each of my new WOW friends. I wonder what they are doing and how their day is going, and I quietly bless them wherever they are. Each person in my class is a leader and courageous entrepreneur with their own unique brilliance. It is the most wonderful incredible feeling to just let the love flow in every direction whether deserved or not. Just let it be. This is what we are all meant to do. We are designed to deliver God's love to anyone that will accept it. What I've found is that most people don't want it. They don't understand it. They are actually afraid of it.

What about the development of my public speaking skills? Oh yeah! I have preached three times since I attended the WOW Factor. I no longer use notes to read my sermons. I don't need them. I prepare to speak in a different way now. My heart must understand what I want to say or I cannot say it. I'll just mumble or muddle through it. I'm willing to risk complete failure and embarrassment for the chance to be honest and brilliant. I know God wants that for us all. When I preach to my home congregation, I know I'm preaching to the toughest crowd I'll ever speak to. They know me so well. They know everything about me, and if I can speak to them effectively, I know I can WOW any audience.

My prayer for you is that you let no more time go by without contacting your real and true authentic self. The world needs to hear from you, because you are great! We need you. Start your journey today and let me hear from you. I hope you will continue on your quiet path to enlightenment and self-discovery. You are the unfolding of the universe, the undoing of time and human suffering. You are the one we are all waiting for. I've never met you, but I know you because I know me. I believe we all share a common humanity. We share such a huge commonality, a communion of the soul, and sense of fear, hesitation, shyness, meekness, and, for many of us, a desire to stay quietly in the background of our social situation. But your contribution is needed. You are here because the universe has already chosen to express itself through you. You are an integral part of an unfolding cosmos. We simply don't always perceive the delicate threads that connect us to one other. They are invisible cords and strands of life and light and spirit that weave through the fabric of each human being. If you remain in the shadows and pass from this earth without sharing your brilliance, we will all lead poorer lives because we didn't get to know you. DO SOMETHING NOW!

The Dark Night of the Soul

"You can search throughout the entire universe for someone who is more deserving of your love and affection than you yourself, and that person is not to be found anywhere. You yourself, as much as anybody in the entire universe deserve your love and affection." —The Buddha

We all have moments where we are in doubt, moments of uncertainty, moments when we are not in control. During these times we seem to lose our bearing. Our moral compass points in all directions at the same time and we drift in a sea of confusion and darkness. These are times when our heart skips a beat, our brain slips a gear, and we fall downhill at an ever increasing pace. Sometimes these moments pass quickly and other times we keep falling all the way to the bottom of the stairs. In our most desperate moments of aloneness we feel abandoned in this world. We experience total loss of meaning for our lives, a profound odor of Déjà vu awareness. It is a sonnet describing the complete absurdity of everything!

When the lights begin to dim and the horizon closes in on me so that I can't even focus on what is right in front of me, my mind slips into neutral, and I settle in for a long siege against my heart and soul. The cell door slams shut and I'm alone, without traction sliding into the depths of a dark depression. It seems like someone turned the lights off and pulled the rug from under my feet at the same time. All of this happens in an instant sometimes or more slowly over a few days one slice at a time. I choke on the seeming rejection, the indifference, the lack of energy, the sense of hopelessness of life in this world. It causes me to ask, "Why was I ever born? What does my life mean anyway? When do we get to that place in life where we're supposed to be; the place where we make a positive contribution to the whole human effort?" And so begins another grueling death march through the valley of the shadow of death complete with hungry vultures lurking and peering at every turn in the trail, waiting to pick the last few scraps from what's left of me.

Christianity refers to these periods as "the dark night of the soul." These are periods of overwhelming abandonment, despair, isolation, hopelessness, depression, and a sense that we are utter and complete failures as human beings. And worse, we are not loved by God. We are so bad even Jesus Christ on the cross can't save us. The product of such heartfelt angst is an inner struggle of the forces of good and evil and our very hearts are the battleground where this war is waged- won or lost. This is the stage set for a desperate drama between the known and the unknown, between what we remember and what we have forgotten, between the selfish and the selfless, between our own good and evil. There are things buried deep in our hearts like ancient scars that never quite healed. Many of them are hurtful and traumatic, embarrassing and uncomfortable. We don't remember the agony of the moment we received the wound. It could have been a look from a parent, a cross word, or a moment of shaming. No one could ever recount that moment in time. And so these wounds fester on in us as ghosts and phantoms that drain energy, stalk us constantly in our thoughts and dreams, in the very way we see life. They are not quite there, never seen or heard, but vaguely felt as if half-remembered in a slumber. Sometimes we are acutely aware of the exact moment the arrow enters the heart and shatters it, but then, we think we heal and we don't. It festers and we limp along half asleep in a day dream for many years or for the rest of our life.

I'm never fully aware of the transition I make to the valley of the shadow of death, only vaguely aware. Sometimes, I just wake up there, suddenly, in an instant. It's like a gigantic cosmic rubber band sucks me back into darkness and there I am, just like I left it before, just like it always is. It is the same place. Before me is a sea of hopelessness, an ocean of meaninglessness, a sky of infinite immeasurability, and I am once again a veritable tabula rasa. I am Sisyphus at the bottom of the hill again and again and again. I'm caught in a Samsara night and I have no good Karma left. Somewhere in my emotional DNA are the detailed instructions for me to get back to the valley of the shadow of death. I'm not sure how I learned to go there or when I first started going there, but my personal emotional DNA works like a Swiss watch every single time.

The valley of the shadow of death is familiar territory. I've walked too many miles through it already and I always come out the other side. It's the place where I work out my destiny, where I am patient for God and I listen. It's the trip to the valley that always deflates me. I hang on as long as possible, lose my grip on sanity, and then, I'm back in that place. I guess I mostly begrudge the slide into oblivion rather than living in the oblivion probably because of the sense of loss during the slide. It's as if I reach a point where I'm almost good, almost a normal human being, and then bam- the great slide back to the valley. Maybe my time up on top is only another aspect of my daydream. Once I hit bottom I realize I have no place lower to go. I can stay here a while, walk through the valley or start looking for a way out. Sometimes it feels good to wallow around in my own personal tragedy. That's what some of us need once in a while. I've learned there are many ways out of the valley, but sheer time always works for me. Once I get out and back up topside life looks better, I get a little confidence and start the cycle all over again. Sisyphus at the top of the mountain as if I'd actually won!

There are so many great blessings for me in the valley of the shadow of death. For one thing, life on top isn't easy. It's not all roses and sunshine. There is no happiness without sadness, no yin without yang, no up without a down. You have to have a positive mental outlook, but you can't just fake it for very long. They are blessings in that if I'm not challenged I will never grow. When I think about all the times my life was easy I can see there wasn't much learning going on. Conversely, when I remember the traumas, heartbreaks, and struggles I've been through, I see those were the times I dug deep into my heart and soul to get through the mess. Afterwards I could see and feel the growth. Down here I've learned to appreciate my suffering & struggle as necessary tools to teach me how to see more clearly and to grow. Living in the valley of the shadow of death is a place of continual personal challenges that must be faced, accessed, and overcome for my journey to continue. The day I quit walking in the valley is the day I cease to exist.

When Christ calls to you, he calls you to himself, forever, but he calls you to enter into him through your own death. Jesus Christ will be the end of you! He calls us into the fullness of His kingdom, into eternity, but the road to eternity is not easy. It requires us to give up everything, to drop everything we don't need and to trust God. We are called to be the fools in this world, to be holy clowns for Christ's sake! Yes. It's true. It's absolutely true and wonderful and marvelous and gracious and beautiful. The true road to understanding ourselves is the narrow road, the almost impassable road, the road where danger lurks at every turn. It's full of all kinds of uncertainties and our constant companions are doubt and fear.

In the valley of the shadow of death we are tested by fire and all false teachings and beliefs are burned up so we are purged and cleansed of the illusions we cling to. They just don't work there. Our hearts and spirits are weighed and measured to determine if we are fit to return to the world of the living. Our minds sort out the meaningless from the meaningful and we render a value to that which is before us. This is exactly the forum where it's possible to for us to meet God. We will never accept Him up above when our lives are cruising along in our daydream. We think we don't need Him. We think He's not real, but not down here! Stay down here long enough and He becomes our friend, our buddy, our compadre! He's the only one that ever really understands us for who we are. The minute we get back on top it, "Thank you Jesus! I got it from here." And off we go careening down the path of life under our own power again.

It is nearly impossible for modern society to warm up to the concept of God, let alone want to seek Him out, or actually suspect he might be real. Our worldview has become so pedantic and narcissistic we could never find an appropriate perspective to even entertain the notion that something or someone could exist greater than ourselves. The new social consciousness is now lord and master of us all. We are kings of the media, middle earth, and what's happening now.

The people of the twenty first century have developed an all-consuming egocentric view of the universe to the point that we can no longer foster ideas about romance, about mystery, about life's simple pleasures, about the human virtues we once valued.

There is no more time for reverence for anything except our own self. The cold calculating eye of science is our god now and such a convenient god because it doesn't require any personal commitment beyond faithfully gathering the data. Only the evidence is important! There are few rules, a little discipline, and mostly the cold logic of an overblown ego that deals with a specific set of data and ignores the rest of the creature.

The problem with science as a world view is that it always dissects everything. We are always looking for smaller and smaller bits of data as if we can determine the whole from the sum of its parts. It's a fine system for exploring physical reality, but it doesn't answer the theory of everything. It doesn't help us understand who we are in the cosmos. Today, we can pick and choose whatever we like and leave the rest because everything is relative. Scientific reality (could there be any other kind?) is like ordering at McDonalds or Chipotle. If there is no God, no advanced civilization that planted us here, no other discovered inhabitants in the known universe or any tangible evidence that they even exist, then we must be the highest form of life we know. And if that's true, what does it mean? Do we even care what it means?

In spite of science and God, we are all required to show up every day and live our life. We have to do something and our actions are always based on what we believe about our self and who we think we are. For so many of us, stumbling through failure after failure in life, leaves us winded and confused about who we think we are and what we're worth as a living, breathing human being. Some people have already resolved themselves to failure and self-worth goes out the window. What if we could find a way to pick ourselves up and start over? What if we could just let go of all our past failures and take our life in a different direction? Resurrection is that thing that grants us power to shift gears, change directions, and begin a whole new venue of self-discovery. We do not need to be the sum total of our past. We have the power to reinvent who we are, or more precisely, to discover our authentic self and the real person we have always been. Resurrection is a verb we employ to reinvent ourselves and become new. It is our new future starting right now!

When people visit the valley of the shadow of death nowadays, it is not to resolve some profound moral dilemma. It's because we're out of cash or out of credit. It's because our Facebook page is not right, not working, not bringing us the ROI we expected. It seems we have become a morally bankrupt society and are now adrift in a sea of social unrest. We are Israel wandering in the desert trying to get to the Promised Land and bitching the whole time. There is not one strong thing or ideal we can tether to in the great storm that is engulfs us. There are no more ideals or absolutes. Everything now is relative. We all drift like little boats tossed in a storm, searching for temporary shelter and finding none. People wonder and ask, "Where is our God? How long must we endure these times?"

The Old Testament in Ecclesiastes 1:2-11 says, *"Vanity of vanities, says the Preacher, vanity of vanities! All is vanity. What does man gain by all the toil at which he toils under the sun? A generation goes and a generation comes, but the earth remains forever. The sun rises and the sun goes down, and hastens to the place where it rises. The wind blows to the south and goes round to the north; round and round goes the wind, and on its circuits the wind returns.*

All streams run to the sea, but the sea is not full; to the place where the streams flows, there they flow again. All things are full of weariness; a man cannot utter it; the eye is not satisfied with seeing, nor the ear filled with hearing. What has been is what will be, and what has been done is what will be done; and there is nothing new under the sun. Is there a thing of which it is said 'See this is new'? It has been already, in the ages before us. There is no remembrance of former things, nor there any remembrance of later things yet to happen among those who come after."

These words were written several thousand years ago, yet they are as relevant today as they were then. We seem to have lost our ability to play at life, to be children, to make mistakes, to be fully human. That is the whole point of being here, in this place, to enjoy it, to appreciate it with a sense of wonderment and a sense of humor for the mystery and unknowing, not believing for a moment we are bigger than this place. It is Mother Earth and we are little more than ants crawling around on it for no amount of time at all and then we're dead! The only hope I see for myself and for all of us is to let go of this insanity and just let it float downstream. We will actually be okay. We will survive if the mail doesn't come tomorrow. The real world will not end, only the imaginary world based upon time kept by the atomic clock. Each of us perpetuates the myth of the atomic time clock. We make it real by obeying it and conforming to it. This will lead to more failure, more human misery and the loss of self for billions of people.

In the valley of the shadow of death all things are possible. It is the crucible of the soul and the place where our hearts are made whole. Solitude is possible. It is even possible to hear "the still small voice of the Lord" in that place. It is our last refuge from the matrix of insanity we have created for everyone. It is the place where the spirit meets the flesh and the marriage of heaven and earth is performed. Everyone needs to visit the valley and live there as long as it takes to come out whole and authentic at the other end. It is the place where we suffer and then make our suffering count for something better, for a higher purpose of expression. It is only when all seven billion of us decide to live into our authentic selves that this world will actually start delivering the potential it is capable of. The first step must be to decide to make the inner journey to the self which resides deep within our own heart. It is the most perilous and treacherous journey a person can make. We will be our own worst enemies during the journey for we have been the prison guards of this place our whole lives. It has been a forbidden place. There is an ocean of childhood trauma that must be processed and discharged and we will need the heart of a lion to face it and deal with it. Lao Tzu says, *"To know yet to think that one does not know is best; Not to know yet to think that one knows will lead to difficulties."* In this place, it's best to let God lead you by the hand through it. We mostly don't make it alone.

Society teaches us at an early age to put on a false face and pretend to be someone we are not so we can play the game. Society also dictates what's important to us and so it sets our personal values. Before that we only had family values and family values are where we got our first instructions on who we are. We never had a chance. All infants are captives of their parents and must conform to the desires and needs of the parents if they hope to survive in this world. We were never taught this, but we learned it anyway. Amazing how the human mind works; learning without teaching.

Life as a human being, a fully alive, fully actualized human being, requires struggle and having courage and to never quit fighting to work through all the values we've accumulated and to evaluate them and test them and throw away any of them that don't work. We all think we're individuals and have fooled ourselves into believing we've stumbled upon our authentic selves. We are mostly the products of our parents and the cultural values that were prevalent at the time of our growing up. That's the sum of who we are unless we make the most of our time in the valley of the shadow of death experience and allow it to bring us to the present moment. In each present moment there exists the great crucible of truth that weighs us and measures us and in this brief moment, there exists a way out, a doorway opens for us. We have the capacity, the ability to be free, to break free, or to remain once again a prisoner of our history, but only in this moment. If we don't do it now, we never will.

The Myth of Jesus

"O Jerusalem, Jerusalem, killing the prophets and stoning those who are sent to you! How often would I have gathered your children together as a hen gathers her brood under her wings, and you would not! Behold, your house is forsaken. And I tell you, you will not see me until you say, 'Blessed is he who comes in the name of the Lord'!" –Luke 13:34-35

When I wake up each morning, it's still dark, but I see the light of day coming soon. I notice the crows already gathered outside my window, waiting, looking around, getting organized for the day's activities, and smacking their beaks in anticipation of a meal. The blood in my veins has dried up hard as caked dirt during the night rendering my body nearly lifeless. I can only manage a couple of breaths and feel the blood flowing immediately, but ever so slowly down my legs. As I squirm and stretch in bed I get a sense for what parts are still numb, still without any flowing blood, and what I'm left to work with. Incredibly, as if by magic or by some unknown force or the urgency of my work schedule, I throw off the covers, get out of bed, and stand on my own! The floor is cold, the room is cold, but I'm up!

One more time I escape from the slumber of the tomb and emerge into the world of the morning. The night thoughts, fears, uncertainties, and other things slink back into their dark place and rest patiently for me to return at the end of my day. I would prefer hot lava to come out of my showerhead to warm me, but settle for the regular steaming hot water. It works every single day to wake me up, put heat and energy in my body and helps send me on my appointed rounds.

I grab my stuff; briefcase, lunch, and mug of coffee, bid farewell to my wife and two dogs and step out into the early morning light wondering how much of my brain the crows will get at today. They're always happy to grab a little snack. A beakful is all they ever demand or even expect as if it's their due and somehow it's my cosmic responsibility to let them have it for the toll that must be paid each day. "Go ahead", I think…"I don't really need it anyway and besides, there's not much left and when it's gone, where will you go, who will feed you then?" It doesn't matter. Hahahaha! Me without a brain and them without food! Everything works out for the best in this life.

As I drive down highway 99 each morning listening to the news on the radio, my mind shifts from the news reports to my morning ritual of asking God for help. "Let me cause no harm today. Let my words be few and kind. Help me God to do good today with whatever it is I'm supposed to do. Help me to be encouraging to people today." That's it. I say it over and over a few more times adding some stuff here and there. With my morning prayers said, the coffee is going down smooth, I notice the highway is filled with crazy people weaving in and out of traffic because they didn't get up in time and are now making up precious moments at the expense of everyone's safety.

The road must be filled with stoned zombies this morning. It is a perfect world and we are all on our way to our day's destiny. It's wonderful to be civilized! Still, there are so many drivers in California that don't fully realize that the left lane on the highway is called "the fast lane" for a reason. At the front of every traffic-jam is some zombie that won't get over and let the rest of us pass. We've come so far as a species, but can't seem to evolve to the point that we all understand that the left lane IS the fast lane! I can sense a connection with the drivers around me that we are all collectively on the cutting edge of a revolutionary evolutionary new beginning and awaiting with hearts on tender hooks for that brilliant moment of new hope to arrive and change life as we know it. Of course I'm talking about winning the lottery. Nobody really believes they'll get rich working for a living. Almost everyone really does hope they win the lottery. None of us like our jobs anymore. We all seem to be in the same sad little boat today.

I haven't always been so optimistic. There have been many dark times in my life, but like dear Candide, breathing life into the brilliant teachings of Dr. Pangloss, I agree that we do live in the best of all possible worlds and these words give me extra hope. It seems like only yesterday I was getting married for the first time and marrying who I thought was the love of my life. It never dawned on me that I was not her knight in shining armor. It didn't take long living happily ever after that we both realized we were not living in the best of all possible worlds. Still we gave it our best shot trying to make it work. Who knows these things or how bad it's supposed to be or can get? It would be only a few short years later when she would deliver us a dead son and both our hearts would shatter into a million pieces never to be whole again and then drift apart forever hoping to pick up the pieces later and who knows, maybe life could be good again. I think it would have been impossible for us to have ever healed had we stayed together. The grief was too great. Did it ever occur to me that I should be more careful about the choices I make, that all things in life are not always what they seem to be? No it didn't. I learned a whole new level of human pain and suffering. - Another poignant lesson from the good Dr. Pangloss. Suffering is necessary to teach empathy.

That's how I came to renounce my faith, quit the seminary, turn my back on the church, and reject the absurd reign of God and all his empty promises. He could keep them, keep his church, and keep everything else that belonged to him. How could I have ever thought I could serve Him and His church? It was only a ruse, a pretense, a cunning way for me to drop my guard and open my heart to the fullness of life, to my hopes, and my dreams. I was done with it! I spent the next few decades proving the valuable truth that Dr. Pangloss taught Candide and that's how I came to understand that we really do live in the best of all possible worlds.

Even pain in the present circumstance plays a useful service toward creating a happy ending. A whole new world opened up for me filled with bars, women, drugs, and everything else a man needs to forget his problems. The whole affair was a whirlwind of good times, bad times, fast times, running up a cosmic karmic bar tab and never considering how I would pay for it all. It didn't matter. I figured I'd stick someone else with my share of the tab or weasel out of it some other way. It was fun. I didn't merely wander in the desert of despair, but stumbled and fumbled my way from one pathetic day to another, coveting and sheltering the gaping wound in my heart and pretending it wasn't there. I was a dead man, but I didn't know it. I was a crazy man, but I didn't know it.

For some of us the cruel tutelage of life's lessons appears to be more than we are ever willing to pay. Some of us are so poor, so pathetic we can't afford to pay attention to the small but important details of our own lives and rather than seek shelter for the emotionally infirm, I continued on stage as if I was somehow the star of the show! Hahahaha! Me with a big smile on my face, tap dancing on the hearts of others as if I'd actually won. In the end, I slithered off into the darkness as a broken man to heal up as best I could.

Not all the days and years of my lost decades of self-imposed exile and banishment from my sanity were wasted wandering hopelessly in darkness. God in His infinite mercy never leaves us even when we quit Him. I didn't go to church. I didn't pray. I didn't ask Him for a single thing for fifteen years, but He took care of me every step anyway. During these years I developed a love of philosophy, music, history, literature, art, theater, and dance. I spent three years as a ballet dancer and while I was never any good at all, I loved it. I love the hard work and focus and discipline a dancer must endure and be willing to inflict upon their mind and body to deliver the exquisite expressions of truth and beauty they offer in a few fleeting movements. I marveled at the women I studied with. They were so gracious and accepting of me. They were strong willed with strong bodies and every bit the physical warrior. I was the only man in the studio. One thing I learned studying ballet with so many women: after a couple hours of dancing, they smell just like men! Life is beautiful and again I thank Dr. Pangloss for guiding me.

Eventually I washed ashore on the holy land. It wasn't planned or foreseen. It just happened in time, in its own time as almost everything does. This time it was another domestic scene that drove me back into the church. After spending 12 weeks in some kind of Catholic boot-camp for wayward couples and after hours and hours of soul wrenching prayer, I became reacquainted with the habit of talking with God. I knew clearly that it was His Hand on the rudder of my life, although I was ashamed to acknowledge it, and presently He was guiding my shipwrecked soul into calmer waters although I had no clue where I was going. I'm not sure how I ever managed the energy to drag myself away from such a quagmire of misery. I don't blame my wife. It wasn't her fault. It never was. It's always my fault for being thoughtless, for not thinking the whole thing through, for not having the personal resources for the both of us, for not being a better man, husband, father, human being. I was better off alone and so was she. This was my current situation, but I truly did not understand it as such. Somehow I managed to slither away and ended up alone in my Grandma's old house. This was my other grandma-my Irish party grandma with red hair. The road had led me back home to the best of all possible worlds!

I remember putting the key in the door, opening it up, and stepping inside all by myself. An ancient aroma flooded me with memories from fifty, sixty, a hundred years ago. I had always known those smells as long as I've lived. It was a thick musty smell of aquariums, potted plants, cigarette smoke, whiskey, gin, scotch, beer, wine and every other flavor of alcohol known to man from the ten million parties my Grandma had in her little place, and also, I think, a touch of her essence, the smell of her lingering presence, her personal aroma. I had grown up in this home through a series of many visits. This little broken down one bedroom shack embraced me! My grandmother embraced me1 I could feel her right there with me in every crack, board, fabric of carpet, whiff of dank air, and dusty piece of furniture. I was home! I was among my own blood! Family blood runs much deeper than we fully understand. I was where I was meant to be. I am barely alive, almost conscious, still breathing, but I'm home. The best part of the experience was unpacking the hundreds and hundreds of books I owned. It was the first thing I did. With every volume I removed from the boxes, it was as if the doorbell rang and another guest arrived! By the end of the night, there was a rousing reunion and full blown party going on with me and my book friends. Being nothing more than a pile of ashes, I was ripe for a new beginning.

It was in this place that I came to understand a deeper meaning of the gospel message of Jesus Christ. I hadn't actually invited him back into my life. It didn't happen all at once. It just started quietly and over a period of months I made my peace with God after 15 years in the belly of the beast and wandering like a madman through the desert! I was 42 years old, alone and living in a 700 square foot shack in the Tower District. To me it was home. It was a mansion on a hill, a cathedral of solitude. In this place I learned the value of being alone with myself and just letting go of time and being and breathing and not thinking about anything.

The promise I made to myself was to make myself a whole person and not move from this spot until the work was done. The only social outlet for me besides work was church on Sunday. Not having a woman in my life allowed me plenty of time to read and review all the philosophy, literature, eastern philosophy, religions of the world, ancient aliens, ghost stories, tales from the crypt, paranormal accounts, and of course, the Holy Bible.

In all of mythology and all the ancient stories of the world, there is not one story that compares to the myth of Jesus of Nazareth. Most stories have a moral, a lesson, an object, a learning and teaching of some esoteric knowledge passed down from generation to generation. The myth of Jesus is not like that. The point of the story quickly dissolves into the deeper meaning of the narrative and the incredible implication required of the listener. The soulfulness is hard to get on a quick first read. Jesus was the most tragic and triumphant human being that ever lived. He was truly a man of sorrow. It would have been the greatest story in Greek Mythology if he had been Greek.

If you can suspend judgment for a moment and undo all the emotional and sociological references and even ignore the religious training you've been given, and listen with new ears and see with new eyes, it may become possible to cultivate a deeper appreciation for the value of the story and of this man who is God the Beloved. This means moving beyond Jesus as a mere archetype, beyond the idea of a savior, and understanding his role in the universe. It also means moving beyond the experience of having this stuff pounded into your head year after year as a child in a church somewhere.

The myth of Jesus might be stated more accurately as the concept of Jesus or the truth about Jesus except for the prejudice the words "concept" and "truth" evokes in the listener. This is not the quadratic equation truth. It is not the unified field theory (concept). It is a more subtle and elegant truth, a deeply profound prayer about being. We have been taught and learned to presuppose we are aware enough and possess the skills and intellectual tools to divine the truth about God. We don't! We can't! We don't have the capacity to comprehend infinities! We just don't and anyone that tells you different is grasping at suppositions and slinging theories, hypotheses, and equations around like they know what they're talking about. All our science and knowledge is nothing but a collection of "how to" manuals about how things work. They don't have the scope to define all meaning everywhere in the universe. Science cannot produce a grand theory of everything! These things only describe apparent physical aspects of the universe and mostly of things found here on Earth. Our greatest scientists don't know how it all started. They don't know why. There is such an incredible black hole of knowledge that is still unknown and perhaps forever unknowable. We accept the unanswered questions on faith, hoping someday we will have the skills and the tools to gain the answers. In the meantime, we have theories and hypotheses as in hypothetical. Such is the hope and faith of our science. We can enjoy all the faith in science we want to, but it's somehow naïve and silly to have any faith in God? In the end, the Mind of God is unknowable and so this debate will rage on forever. Jesus can be understood only in the heart and specifically a desperate heart, a pathetic heart, a broken heart.

We've developed the habit over the centuries to press onward and upward in our quest to know everything there is to know and believe we already know it! Actually every age thinks they've cracked the code and solved the mysteries of the universe. Certainly the contributions Pythagoras made to astronomy and mathematics catapulted mankind into a new age of understanding. Between Pythagoras and Aristotle we all came to understand the universe revolved around the earth. This was common knowledge several hundred years ago. But science like everything else on earth evolves and changes into something else. Years later Nicholas Copernicus offered a more reasonable solution to astronomers everywhere. He believed, and rightly so, that the earth was not the center of the universe. It was the sun that seemed to be the exact center of the universe. He was not alone in his ideas. Galileo and Kepler embraced the wisdom of Copernicus and it seemed all scientific knowledge came to understand that the sun is actually the center of the universe and not the earth as the church believed based only on a couple of misquoted bible passages.

I don't believe for one minute that the earth or the sun is the center of the universe! I'm not sure exactly where the center is. I guess I'd need to know where the outer edges are if I were going to try and determine where the exact center might be. And if we're all spinning round and round and if everything is only relative anyway, what does it really matter where the center is? It only ever matters what we can know as individuals. I tend to think I must be the very center of the universe. I'm pretty sure I am anyway. I mean, what can I ever know for sure? I'm having a hard time knowing myself, but at least that is an attainable possibility! And if I can't even know who I am, how can I ever hope to know anything else? And you, you must believe you are the center of the universe as well. Why not? This is not an absolute scientific certainty, but maybe, it is all we can ever know as individuals, as a person. Everything now is relative, so we can all have our truth custom made. Every so often, some smart person stumbles on a crumb of truth that changes all the heretofore "truths" as we've come to believe them, and we collectively embrace "the new truth."

Not even a hundred years later Isaac Newton arrives on the scene and changes everything again, forever! By this time, the church has been shredded of just about everything respectable and believable and Newton and science emerge as the new gods of mankind. It has been so ever since. We all now know that the universe knows no greater power and authority than the fruits of the mind of man. We are god now in this place! By the time Friedrich Nietzsche comes around, he is aghast at what educated men have dreamed up. The meaning of their thoughts and words offer a mortal wound to the man of vision and compassion. His words whispered in our ear ushers us all into the mind of modern man, the post nihilistic age beyond reason, beyond sanity.

We are now un-tethered from God. Our absolute values are gone and replaced with relative values that go up and down from moment to moment. Life is now a sterile laboratory where we can concoct any brew that suits us. He saw it all coming from such a long way off. By the time we put together the Manhattan Project Team and their new invention, science had shown mankind the door and we are on our way to the best of all possible worlds! It matters not whether it's the visible church on earth or even the brilliance of the scientific mind, the political mind, or the national pride mind. We all began to move together toward a kind of weird social madness that suggested we had already learned enough to the point that we know almost everything.

But none of this matters at all. No one remembers this stuff. We don't even care! There is nothing in front of us right now except whatever the latest pop culture topic is serving up as fashionable. It is in exactly this moment in time that Jesus of Nazareth may have some shred of relevance for us. Our social systems seem to have broken down. We've killed the idea that the Christian church or any church for that matter can do any good anywhere. We are fast learning that no matter whether democrat or republican, we cannot support the world forever or buy everything the world makes forever. We cannot print money forever and must somehow come to terms with some sort of life discipline. The good news in all of this: we have come to the place in the trail where we have little else to lose except our freedom and our dreams. There is not much more downside from the poverty of this madness except to do nothing and fuel its continued existence and then, what do we say to our children? What do we tell them on the day they ask us why? What legacy do we leave for our children who come after us? What does this say about who we are? That we were spiritually bankrupt? That we had drawn down the spiritual bank account down to zero and then some? We are all orphans in this place now.

If God is God, wouldn't He create the best of all possible worlds as our dear Dr. Pangloss proposes, or would He or could He create an inferior world? There would be no purpose to create anything less than the best of all possible worlds. The best of all possible worlds would necessarily include the creation of sentient beings (us) and giving them the true ability to choose good or evil. (Free moral choice) Any world where the sentient beings did not actually have free moral choice would be an inferior world. God could set up an actual world where his sentient beings actually had free moral choice and which, while he being Omniscient would know the outcome, could nevertheless allow his creatures to have actual free moral choice. And this is exactly what he did! The bigger question is: If every person is endowed with a soul made by God and is part of God, how could that soul ever be separated from God forever? How can hell exist?

There would be no purpose for God to create an inferior world where his sentient beings did not have actual free moral choice. So God created us with actual free moral choice to choose between good and evil knowing we would choose evil. God, knowing this beforehand, made provisions for his creatures to be redeemed from their poor choice when they eventually chose evil. The terms for this provision "the Atonement" or "The Redemption of Creation". In the most incredible way conceived, God made provision to send his Son to live among His creatures as one of them and to live in His Creation without sinning or always choosing the good and never choosing evil, and then to create the atonement for us all. It is through the righteousness of Jesus that God creates the reconnection between us and Himself. If God doesn't love us, then all bets are off. The death and resurrection of Jesus is God's sacrifice of Himself to us as a demonstration of unconditional love. What more evidence does a person need to believe God loves them? In this action, God has created a superior world, the best of all possible worlds in that His fallen creatures can choose to love him and their love is genuine, true, authentic, and real. It is the only kind of love that matters.

How do we know this to be true? It is our experience of love. A mother always loves her child. She loves her babies without any conditions at all by virtue that she carried them, birthed them into the world, and nurtured them to maturity. A mother loves her babies without question for who they are. A husband loves his wife, his children by virtue of who they are. Brothers, sisters, cousins, friends, all love each other because of who they are. Even devil worshipers want to be loved! Even atheists believe in love! Of course many people love others for what they can give them. This is not the same kind of love. Anyone sharing tender moments with others intuitively understands the depth of meanings that exist in the human heart and during tender moments in our existence. All human value exists in this organ, in this soul, in this spirit. It cannot be quenched or stilled. It is! The human heart is the most complex organ in the body. It holds the most ghastly things and at the same time, the most tender thoughts and feelings and the very meaning of human life.

My aim is to bring you to this point where your mind can consider an alternative to the cerebral treatment of such an important subject as the nature of God. It is not an easy or light subject. If you have determined to an absolute certainty that God could not exist and does not exist, then read no further. My words will be meaningless to you. If there is a slight doubt or curiosity, then please proceed. All this preparation and pretense is necessary to set the stage, to prepare the palate of mind and heart to open the door, to wake up the soul, to prepare the spirit to receive understanding of things not seen.

The myth of Jesus is not a myth at all. To believe in the truth of Jesus one must become as a madman in this world. It is an experiential truth that in the end, you believe or you don't believe. It's an individual choice. Many of the values in this world do not translate well into the realm of the eternal or of understanding infinities of any type. Our social rules govern everything in this place, and are based on a quid pro quo relationship for everything. There must be "something for something" or there's no social exchange, no gain nor loss; there is no transaction. This is not second nature to us; it is our first nature. We all comprehend quid pro quo without any explanation at all. It's the law of commerce, the barter system, the exchange of something for something. We have something we don't need and someone has something we need. If the exchange is agreeable to both, the transaction occurs to the satisfaction of both parties. The grace of God does not work this way.

With respect to the previous discussion, it is easy to understand that God would not create a world where true freedom of will did not exist. God knew before He created us that we would fall. He had to! People think of God as being a detached and indifferent far way God, someone who doesn't know us or understand us. God is not this way at all. He sent his Son Jesus to live as a man, a real man in a frail human body, to live among us as one of us. If you read the Old Testament you will find numerous passages that proclaim the coming of God's Son, the Holy One. These books were written hundreds of years before Jesus had been born. There is independent corroboration through verification of the records of The Dead Sea Scrolls. They can be scientifically verified as existing before Jesus was born, written from hundreds of years of oral tradition, not unlike the works of Homer, not unlike the works of Pythagoras or Socrates.

Isn't it ironic that the Son of God would be conceived by an unmarried woman? Scandalous! It is insane that the Creator of the Universe would be born in a stable with common cattle and placed in a feeding trough for a bed. So unfitting for the King of Kings! Why would God choose such a place in time to bring His Son into the world? Jesus was completely obscure. He barely learned a trade. He wasn't really successful at it. He wasn't a successful citizen. He didn't own a home. He didn't write a book. He chose his disciples poorly. They were a bunch of marginalized peasants with no education or class at all. Yet, everything written about him suggests he professed a simple, yet profound love....the love of God for His children. Jesus never said he was the Son of God. He said he was the Son of Man. He was labeled a drunkard and a glutton. He associated with prostitutes, tax collectors, and every other marginalized social class of the time. He hung out with losers and people with zero political power. The only people Jesus ever challenged were the rich and the righteous. He challenged them to be whole people and not trust in their riches and positions. He challenged them to be caring and share of their hearts and souls, but they could not because they had already amassed so much wealth and power. How could they give up such things to go down in their station and associate with the common masses? Jesus spoke out against the so-called religious people, the good people of his day, but he knew they would not listen to him because they were absorbed with their own position in life, their own truth.

The focal point of his ministry was to serve the down-trodden, the hopeless. He knew he could do nothing for the religious and the rich. When the authorities, both religious and political pressed him, he didn't resist. He was arrested. His friends abandoned him. He was beaten and questioned and humiliated and he said nothing. And then he was crucified in front of the entire known world. There was no press coverage, no historians, but only the local townsfolk. It just happened. He was nailed up on a cross, naked and abandoned and all he did was ask a question and pray that his executioners be forgiven for what they had done. The only thing he muttered was, "Father, forgive them for they know not what they are doing" and "My God! My God! Why have you forsaken me?" If you can consider for one moment this profound scene, where the Son of God, where God Himself is abandoned, bleeding and beaten on a cross by his own Creation in order to reconcile all of us to Himself, then you can begin to see the passion of God for his children. He died and was buried in the tomb of a follower. It was done. The so-called Messiah had come and gone and nothing was any different. The Roman Empire had executed a known criminal and it was now a matter of public record. It was an historical fact. This was done that everyone throughout history might know that God does not work in the dark. He works in the light for all to see.

The body of Jesus was taken to the tomb of Joseph of Arimathia, a known member of the Sanhedrin. There were Roman guards placed in front of the tomb to keep anyone from stealing the body. Yet three days after his crucifixion, the tomb is found empty. The Roman guards had no idea what happened, and the body of Jesus is gone! You have to wonder what happened to those guards that let this thing happen. They were probably executed. On numerous occasions after this hundreds of witness's state they saw the living Jesus sporting His wounds! For several weeks after his crucifixion Jesus continued to appear to his followers. It's interesting to note that the followers of Jesus hid out after His death. They were terrified and despondent that their leader had been killed. They had no clue as to what to do next, but they stayed together until......until...... Jesus appeared to them, alive! Immediately after that they went into the streets and proclaimed Jesus as the Messiah and the Son of God. Before this, they were defeated, terrified, frozen with fear, and now under exactly the same conditions, they stepped out and spoke out. What had changed? They were beaten and jailed, but they did not stop proclaiming the gospel!! The light of truth can never be hidden. It is the light shining in the dark. The question we must ask ourselves is this: Is God capable of doing this?

The deeper meaning of all this discussion has to do with only this; God asks us to search our hearts for the true being He created us to be. Many of us figure that our solitary life doesn't amount to much in this world. We are the quiet ones, the ones who just get along. Yet, we are the ones that God chooses to bring into being that which was not. He chooses us to express his divine comedy, His divine tragedy, and all the folly that falls between the two extremes. This is life. This is what it means to be human. We are suspended somewhere between nothing and heaven, between emptiness and fullness.

Oh yes! I went on to marry a wonderful woman with two fantastic children. They loved me very much and I loved them very much. How would I have known the value of such things had I not experienced the tragedies of my previous life? How does one ever know the value of anything unless it can be compared to another thing? We never quite know when life gives us unexpected treasures and sometimes even the meaning of life itself. And from all of this I learned that Dr. Pangloss was exactly right: we do live in the best of all possible worlds!

GraceLand

"There are times when we become acutely aware of human frailty, moments that contrast what we can and cannot do. In an instant nature changes everything we've ever known to be true and we believe we are alone in the cosmos. Our rock solid foundation of knowledge evaporates in the experience of living in seeming chaos leaving us helpless victims."-Richard R. Smith

Our world is a very unforgiving place. It's full of manmade rules and regulations, laws and penalties. In America, not knowing the law is not an excuse. Some of us commit crimes out of ignorance or carelessness, but we don't get caught. There are others around us that purposely violate the laws of the land with a willful intent to do harm to someone. They commit murder, theft, rape, mayhem, arson, crimes of passion, and treason. These people are the enemies of society, the one's that, for one reason or another, did not assimilate into the social fabric of our value system. How does a society produce a criminal? What is our role as responsible citizens to help prevent people from becoming criminals? Can criminals be cured? Is it enough to simply punish them? Is there any sense of forgiveness or grace for a convicted criminal? Is there ever much difference between a criminal and the rest of us?

As if our own manmade tragedies were not enough, we all suffer through the often violent outbreaks of nature that catch us aware and unprepared to experience such loss of life, such widespread grief. From time to time, we take short breaks from killing each other to help those that have been killed and wounded by nature. It doesn't matter if it's a tsunami, a tornado, an earthquake, a virus, or even a hungry tiger, we will all band together to help each other when nature's wrath takes human life. There seems to be no reason for such events and most people would not attribute a sense of grace to any of this type of destruction.

One thing I know for sure, if you owe somebody something, they will make you pay what you owe! There will be no forgiveness of debt, no reprieve, no pardon. The law is the law and a deal is a deal! That's just how we roll in this world. The whole point of contract law is to establish a binding agreement or covenant between two consenting adults that defines something for something. It's a quid pro quo arrangement with expectations on both sides of the equation. This all makes sense in a world of commerce, in a social world where we negotiate for whatever it is we need or want. Everyone is expected to keep their end of the bargain or else there's trouble. Humans have a natural penchant for the quid pro quo concept of social life.

Business contracts are easy stuff. Everyone understands them. The confusion starts at the point where the individual person begins to relate to the rest of society. Social responsibility varies from country to country and culture to culture. The social fate of the individual is closely tied to their family history, social and religious values, and most importantly, the level of healthy nurturing a child receives as they are growing up. These factors will play a major role in how successful an individual integrates into the society around them. What constitutes a "model" citizen? How do we define our social obligations to everyone else? Who is everyone else? Do we include family, friends, neighbors, and strangers? Do we owe allegiance to our city, state, country, and the whole world? The bigger question is: Are we really the family of humankind or merely a collection of nations and cultures? Do our socio-political rules trump the rules of nature? How does a single individual fit into such a structure?

There is another force of nature that lives almost under the level of everyday consciousness. It's a lingering collective guilt brought on by our willful apathy when we avoid speaking out against social injustice that promotes inequalities and exploitation of others for the benefit of a few. There is no one to make us do this social work, except our conscience. We all know it's not right to exploit others for personal gain and yet we willingly ignore these situations believing we won't make a difference. We make excuses for inaction because "it's not our business". It's the way we get what we want from those who have it. It's how we get by in the world. This instinct is imprinted in our social DNA. The question becomes for the individual: How much is enough? What do we want and need in order to be happy, to be fulfilled as a human being? There is a hole in our heart so big that no matter what level of success we achieve or how much wealth we accumulate, it's never enough to fill the hole. And in the process, we adopt the idea that the ends justify the means and we become unfaithful to our authentic selves.

Grace: Random House defines it as- clemency, pardon, the freely given unmerited favor and love of God. We all want to be in God's favor, to be loved by Him, but what can we do? We can't earn it. We can't climb our way to heaven. We can't buy a pardon from God. We need grace. If you take grace out of Christianity, it's no longer Christianity. All the other religions of the world have some basis in morality, in human effort, in human works. Christianity works only through the means of grace, that is the grace of God, and specifically, the grace of God in Jesus Christ. Most of us can claim to be model citizens because we haven't done jail time, haven't cheated on our taxes, or haven't made a public nuisance of our self, but that hardly serves as model behavior.

The Christian is required to live by a much higher standard than the citizen, but we mostly don't. If a Christian even thinks a bad thought, it's the same as committing the act. How does anyone get relief from that? We don't! We are forgiven for our errors, our sins, and made whole by grace alone. It is God's grace that saves us all and we Christians are required to show grace to everyone we meet, but we mostly don't. The world is very short on grace. It is the dynamic of something for nothing. It is the act of kindness to the stranger with no hope of repayment. It is committing the act of kindness for the sake of the act.

Love, unconditional love, pursues those who need it most, which are always those who cannot pay for it. From a spiritual perspective, none of us can pay the price.

When I attended the WOW Factor last May, there was a moment when I found myself on the other side of the crusty layer that surrounds my heart. I was on the inside of my heart; the inner sanctum where my heart has not been bruised! I breathed a deep lungful of fresh air and realized instantly I had been suffocating for the last fifty years. For almost my whole life I had not taken a single breath, had not taken a moment to properly question who I am, who I was, who I had become. I thought I had, but I hadn't. That's the beauty of the illusion; it's so believable and real. The dream is so real until something else comes along. It is as if I had awakened from a long sleep, not remembering exactly when I had dozed off. When grace comes to us it illuminates all the dark corners of our lives and reaches deep into our prenatal consciousness where we all once lived and we begin to get a sense for how far we've fallen. For many of us our mother's womb may very well be the last address where we felt whole, fully loved, and fully alive. Grace washes over us and sweeps us back into that small interior space of warmth, acceptance, validity, and purpose. We are illuminated by the glow of our prenatal consciousness and sense of being. It is a time before we learned to judge ourselves or measure our failures. We are carried back to a place in time where we were not in charge, where we could simply be and where our self-worth was assumed and didn't need to be earned.

It started out as not more than a tiny spark, a barely noticeable difference in everything. It was like staring east into the inky blackness of the Sierras right before the sun comes. One second there is nothing and the next, a faint outline of peaks in the distance that makes you feel something is coming. The awareness grows into a small flame that began to shed light, allowing me to clearly see the small details of my life. Very soon, I was swept away into a torrent of tears sobbing relentlessly at the horror of my narcissistic self. The image of me grew clearer and clearer as I began to realize how self-absorbed I had always been. I never meant to be that creature standing before me and now remembering how I had invented him so long ago unaware then that he would steal my entire life.

The memories started coming one at a time and then simply flowing at me from the past. I was bleeding out the poison of a lifetime of pretense and today was reckoning day for my heart and soul. The black blood oozed out of every orifice and pore in my body and I could do nothing except watch it happen and try to understand what it meant. Many thoughts, feelings, and memories flooded into my head as I began to understand my failures. I had failed my mother and father, my brothers, sister, aunts, uncles, cousins, my whole family. I had failed all my friends as well. I was never there for them either. In every single way I had made the wrong choice over and over and over again. I was never a very good husband or father for that matter. Almost everything I had ever done ended in ruin. There were so many times that I almost succeeded, almost completed something, but not quite. My whole life was one that could have been something good, but I never quite made it to the finish line.

I stood there in the darkness alone with my past and my thoughts about it and watched the flames grow until the whole structure was ablaze. The house of my persona was being consumed at last, releasing my heart and soul to begin a new journey. Immediately she arrived and picked up my remains and gathered me in her arms with such tender love. I began to cry anew, but this time, they were tears of sheer joy. When grace comes to you, she brings a healing balm and binds up a lifetime of wounds. I didn't deserve it. I haven't earned it. There's nothing any of us can do to earn it. If we are lucky, something happens to us that changes everything and frames our whole life into a new perspective, a divine perspective. Until our very last breathe, each of us has this opportunity to let it all go and claim our authentic self, if even only for a few moments. I am very lucky to have received this gift. I didn't do anything to get it except to give up and go through a kind of death.

It's a real death, a painful death, but also a necessary death. We must each witness the death of the false self of our own creation that we so lovingly made our whole lives to cope with life in this world. That persona is who we think we are and when we allow it to die, there will be mourning for it. When I gave up the pretense of being good and allowed the demons in me full reign, they did what they do; they destroyed everything as quickly as possible, even their own sanctuary. I had almost nothing to do with it except to make one small choice and to stand there and witness it. My job was to accept all of it, to confess my sin, to stand up at last and claim my authentic self.

Grace is that most essential ingredient that rains down cleansing on all of us. It destroys all bragging rights, levels the playing field, and makes us all humble because God knows we will only pick him when we have no picks left to pick. God's grace can only be had by the downtrodden, broken, hopeless, and desperate souls that know they don't deserve it. Nobody else thinks they need it and besides, they are too busy. We all stumble in life. We exploit our foolishness until something stops us. Some of us go to prison while others lose their job or get divorced. Some people get caught and others get away with it. Most of us waste away one day at a time never forgiving ourselves for whatever it was we think we did or didn't do and blaming everyone else because we feel this way.

When grace comes we get a shot at a new life, a new purpose, and sharing our real selves the way God intended us to be. We get something we don't deserve something we haven't earned. We fall headlong into the loving arms of a God that has always been there for us. In the end, eventually, we see clearly how we've wasted the time of our life trusting in things that have no value, believing in schemes that never work. We choke on the loss of so much wasted time and mourn the foolish squandering of the only non-renewable resource we ever own: time. But the dynamic properties of grace change this linear value system when it arrives. In an instant, a wasted lifetime may be reclaimed, infused with a new profound meaning that incorporates all the wasted days into a fresh expression of an authentic self. We spend the time of our life staying busy with stuff that doesn't matter except it distracts us from the important stuff. God never let us very far from his loving embrace, but we don't believe it. We thought we had been abandoned. We end where we began which is not very far from God's loving grace.

There are few moments when I can escape the relentless persecution of my ego and transfer awareness into my heart and be still. When this happens all the power goes out of my head into my heart, and immediately my interior spaces begin to open up. All the hallways and rooms start to unclog and change from darkness into light. It's as if someone opened a window in my soul and let the cool morning breeze drift in. I can feel the connection with heaven, with God. It is an amazing moment when I just let everything go without judgment, without concern, without any thought at all. It's really that easy, but I never think so. I don't believe it's possible. I never believe it's that easy until it happens again. The truth is I don't know how to let go of all the junk I've collected and assigned to its place in my life. This stuff seems so necessary and important. This stuff is the magic ingredient my ego uses to balance all accounts and figure out how I get from here to wherever my ego thinks it wants to take me. It is all the props I need to keep my illusion real and alive. I am not my ego!

The world understands the concept of grace as getting something for nothing or more accurately, getting something you don't deserve. Where we stumble with the concept of grace is realizing the nature of holiness and accepting the idea that God is God and we're not. It's the competitive and comparative spirit of mankind that is inbred in our DNA that compels us to compete and compare ourselves even to God. We just don't want to believe that God is better than us, and so we rationalize that maybe He is a little better, but we're good so He needs to give us a break. It goes even farther in that we think He should slant the deck in our favor and give us what we want.

What we fail to understand or don't want to understand is that God will always give us what we need, but that may not necessarily be what we want. We think God is there to help us get what we want. This presupposes we are smart enough to know what is best for us and we aren't. We want what we want when we want it. And this is antithetical to the concept of grace. It is the unique perspective of the ego existing as a local temporal reality as Deepak Chopra calls it.

The expression of grace can only happen when we've experienced a kind of internal realignment of our priorities and put away the false image of ourselves. In a moment of conviction, our ego is naked and exposed for what it is and we realize this little monster has been lying to us all along. It is not difficult to silence all the voices of the people in our lives. It's almost impossible to silence that internal voice that condemns and criticizes our every move. That voice judges, evaluates, and measures all that I think, say, and do without ceasing. It's the voice of my critical parent I heard long ago and it is now my own personal judge, jury and executioner. It constantly points to a lifetime of failures, disappointments, and fears as telling examples and proof of my worthlessness, and every time I fall, I only have to review my own list for confirmation. It's a pity how shamelessly I use this ammunition to execute my authentic self and snuff out every opportunity for success, for life. Grace is the voice that silences all other voices and it is enough. Grace is sufficient. It pays all the bills and squares up all accounts.

Like refugees from a warzone many of us flock to our little churches every Sunday for healing, for comfort, for rebuilding to prepare ourselves for another week in the trenches. This is not the popular picture of the wealthy, arrogant, and judgmental Christian church most people like to poke fun at. Most of us are simple people that understand we need help. We need God's help and blessings just to make it week after week. And once you, I, and everyone else peel the onionskin down to nothing, we realize our utter helplessness, the complete and total poverty of soul and spirit. We are truly beggars before the cross. I have nowhere else to go in this world, so I go to my church. The sanctuary at my church is really my sanctuary here on earth. I don't know how to get any closer to heaven. In that place I am safe from the storms of life. In that place and among those people, God's grace pours over me and heals me. I can breathe. In that place I have come to understand who I am and what I am and how much I'm worth. I belong to God. He bought me and paid for my life with the life of his Son. I am his beloved and so are you. In the sanctuary of my church I can believe this. That's the message He gave me to share with anyone that will listen. I no longer have the luxury to hide myself in my homespun illusions about who I am. I belong to God and serving Him is all that matters now, but I am such a coward about my assignment. I am coming to understand the gift life gives us back if we but ask for it. It is our self, our real and authentic self that was there all the time hiding, waiting, afraid to come out in the open.

Those outside the Christian church peer inside and wonder how we can believe what we believe. They think it's a naïve faith propped up by 2000 years of tradition. They look at the church and watch what we do and think "they don't really believe it". The skeptics are mostly correct. The church, every church struggles with moral and social issues. We don't always get it right. We Christians sometimes forget what Jesus taught us, which is to love everyone. It's not that easy. It's easy to love those we love, to love those who love us back. It's much harder to love the unlovable people as we've been commanded to love.

For this we are hypocrites, liars, and cowards. We confess our sins and short comings. We get it!

This may be the most appropriate time to discuss other religions and no religions. As a Christian, I have enough faith in God to accept all other religions and even people that have no religion. I'm speaking of atheists here. I have tried many times to be an atheist. I can't say I was an intelligent atheist in that I couldn't roll out all the logical arguments that would prove God does not exist. I just didn't believe there was a God. I can understand how some people feel this way and not believe in God. I can accept this point of view. All of us have many different roads we must travel in our lives and they will all serve us well if we pay attention to the details. Every tree bears fruit of its own kind. Your faith or lack of it will bear the only fruit it can produce. I now understand that when we discover our authentic self, these issues will resolve themselves. I say this because I understand that if God can respect the value of our free will, then the least any of us can do is to follow that example. This means developing a sense of religious tolerance for all religions and knowing that God is in charge of these things.

When I finally decide to make a full court press on my faith, I realized it's not easy at all. It's difficult. It hurts. It's frightening. It's hard. It's impossible! Without Christ, it can't be done! And with that I needed a reintroduction to grace to begin to understand the depth of God's love and commitment to me. My soul began to slowly fill in the blanks about life, about how transitory it all is. I am not more than a breath or two in this place and then I'll be gone. Why shouldn't I live it fully? Why shouldn't I go for it with my whole being? Grace corrects all the errors of our thinking and teaches us to reach deep inside our hearts and start feeling life. God goes before us and prepares our way. He fights our battles and is never far from us. Isaiah 43 says, *"Fear not, for I have redeemed you; I have called you by name, you are mine. When you pass through the waters I will be with you; and through the rivers, they shall not overwhelm you; when you walk through fire you shall not be burned, and the flame shall not consume you."*

Grace…..grace….grace… the very grace of God is a substance we can't taste at first taste. It can't be smelled with a whiff. Its essence must be ingested, taken down deep inside us and breathed into the lungs of our very being and infused into the blood that courses through our whole body and brings life. It must be eaten and consumed by a hungry starving soul, and become part of us to be effective, to fully transform us. This pathetic Jesus that has become the butt of so many jokes was described this way many thousands of years ago. The prophet Isaiah writes in chapter 53:

"Who has believed what we have heard? And to whom has the arm of the Lord been revealed? For he grew up before him like a young plant, and like a root out of dry ground; he had no form or comeliness that we should look at him, and no beauty that we should desire him. He was despised and rejected by men; a man of sorrows, and

acquainted with grief, and as one from whom men hid their faces- he was despised, and we esteemed him not.

Surly he has borne our grief and carried our sorrows; yet we esteemed him as stricken, smitten by God and afflicted. But he was wounded for our transgressions, he was bruised for our iniquities; upon him was the chastisement that made us whole, and with his stripes we are healed. All we like sheep have gone astray; we have turned everyone to his own way; and the Lord has laid on him the iniquity of us all.

He was oppressed, and he was afflicted, yet he opened not his mouth; like a lamb that is led to the slaughter; and like a sheep that before its shearers is dumb, so he opened not his mouth."

These words were passed down by oral tradition and recorded in the Book of Isaiah which is confirmed as one of the Dead Sea Scrolls. These words have a real place in the history of the world and they speak prophetically of the life Jesus lived hundreds of years later. This is the yoke that God gave His Son to bear for us. It is the description of a pathetic man, a rejected man, a scorned man, who came to bring us God's love. How fitting! How utterly and completely fitting that the Creator of the universe would express himself to us with such compassion and tenderness and wisdom? The grace that God gives us is filled with a healing balm, a life-giving ethereal substance that infuses its life force in us and makes us new. What can we do with grace, but drink it in, absorb it, let it kill every impulse and will to self, and pass it on to everyone we meet. It burns us down and humbles us and forces us to look in the mirror and see the true reflection of who we are, who God made us to be.

I'm finally learning to take ownership of all my resentments, hurts, and grudges. I created every one of them and fed them and nurtured them all these years. I chose them to express how I felt at a certain moment in time and they have been loyal companions to me ever since. They have waited patiently for justice to be done, for retribution, or some other silly notion. In the meantime, they have tortured me and tied me down and caused me to suffer. They owned me and my life all these years. I know now that I no longer need them. I claim them as my own and I choose to discard them as useless companions on my life journey. They cannot serve me in any positive way. They are simply a poison that I created when I needed to remember a hurt. I am now in a position where I have learned to look for life lessons every single day and to learn from them to be a better servant.

Grace is ultimately a mystery, a riddle that our modern minds don't fully understand. We accept that every transaction is quid pro quo and nothing is free. This value system does not work with our relationship with God. It's all grace or nothing. You can't buy it. Grace is the means to understanding our place in the universe and our ultimate worth and value as creatures of God. It validates our right to be who we are and where we are in the world. We have a right to be here. We have a purpose to be here in this place at this time. We are part of the whole evolution of the cosmos and have a prominent place in the divine purpose for all creation. This places a level of responsibility on each person to step up and deliver our real authentic self to the cosmic drama of humanity in this world. Grace is a beginning, the starting point on our road to self-discovery and understanding that we are in the world and without it we will never even start the journey.

Ayla and Her Mom

"We start out in life as little children and somewhere along the way we lose ourselves and become somebody else. For a brief period we believe we've won when our children are born, but we haven't. The true test comes when we see our babies having babies. In that moment we return to those magical days when we were children ourselves and life gets so much clearer."

-Richard R. Smith

For most people, daily life finds us actively pursuing our careers either at work, at college, or in the unemployment line. We're busy doing the ordinary everyday things all adults on the planet do for most of our waking lives. It's the business of living of getting by, of hanging on. Despite all the buzz and boredom of the daily, weekly, and monthly routines, there are times when we get to experience the extraordinary, the miraculous, and the beautiful. We look forward to such enriching moments and milestones in our family life. We've planned them a million times, wondered about what "that" will be like one day when it happens, and wait with patient expectation for the day to arrive. There are so many milestones in a family's life.

Some of these magical moments are profound, are more than we expected, and end up affecting us in ways we never anticipated. When this happens, it is as if life itself leads us by the hand pulls back the curtain, and reveals a rich depth of meaning we never knew was possible. We don't know what to feel or how to feel about it. I suppose stunned, enraptured, captivated, humbled, mystified, are words one can use to describe those moments of sheer amazement and gratitude of belonging to each other of holding each other close in the shared moment. Sometimes these moments are so tender that our everyday mind isn't capable of processing the meaning. Life continues to surprise us. Even grandparents! Sometimes we are embarrassed we didn't see it coming.

  I don't know if it was from seeing my granddaughter for the first time or seeing my beautiful daughter calmly and lovingly deliver her baby, but the whole scene left me stunned and looking for something to compare it to and there was nothing. It felt surreal and I was wrapped in a dazzling moment of pure wonderment. The whole scene evoked a visceral response deep inside me complete with decades of past images, sounds, emotions, smells, and memories all flowing into my head and heart in the hospital room. It was like the camera moved in really close for a tight shot and everything had to be just right and perfect and it was! In those focused moments I witnessed the birth of the new generation in my family and saw my daughter bring life from her life! I was not prepared to absorb the meaning of this event. My heart was too small. Seeing my daughter with her baby gave me a glimpse of the future life of our family and showed me how life continues on without us. I was so proud of her and her new baby, my granddaughter.

Sooner or later we must each walk the spiritual gauntlet and give up our illusions and accept the stark vision that truth delivers when she shows up. This usually happens when people we love die, or, when they are born. I know many of us indulge our children and willingly participate in their hopes and dreams because we love them and support them. I have had the privilege of seeing my extraordinary daughter grow up, become a women, take on the challenges of the world, get married, and now….become a mother. I was not prepared to see how she performed this last maneuver with such grace, elegance, heart, character, love, and expression. I am still stunned to see my little girl demonstrate complete control, understanding, inclusion, empathy, grace, and a general knowledge about new babies, motherhood, and life. Seeing her with her new baby, seeing them together at the same time, makes me wonder what they will accomplish together in the next few decades. I think I should shut up, pull up a chair, and try to learn something here. I will be happy if I can just tag along and share life with them.

We all fancy ourselves having the inside edge on life, the unique clear perspective that we know what it's all about and we understand life's potential. We've thought it all out, calculated it, and established our own return on investment. There must be some level of relying on our instincts, trusting our reasoning, values, and ourselves if we are to ever take action in the short life we are given. Many of us stumble through each day caught up in the slick illusion we've created to keep the wolves at bay and sometimes we even make a little progress. Our creative effort mainly serves to breathe life into the daydream that we are actually in control of everything. If we're lucky something happens that slaps that notion out of our head, gives us a few smacks on the bottom and makes us cry. Only then can we move to the heart, turn on the brilliant light we came with, and see this place for what it really is. When this happens we become believers in miracles, believers in the ideas about God's unending love for us, and all of a sudden we know it must be true. We need it to be true because we realize our mortality and our limitations. We see the end of ourselves and begin to realize that life is bigger than we are, and bigger than we thought it was. Our children are blessings to us, but we don't own them, and we need all the help the universe can give us to prosper them. They are the continuation of our lives and of life searching to express itself through them. Seeing the circle of life begin anew and to realize this is where we came in is the joy of a grandparent.

My daughter moved away several years ago and established a new home in Los Angeles. I would not have voted for this option, but she has her own mind, a very strong will, and a clear sense of what she wants. This happened several years ago but the fear and anxiety is still fresh in my heart. Parents will do anything to protect their children, even discourage them from living their dreams, from embracing their destiny, even if it means clipping their wings. I wasn't thinking about such nonsense back then when I drove the U-haul to Los Angeles filled with my daughter's things. She was starting a new life for herself and I, I was in the grips of a massive fear spiral trying to figure out how she was going to stay safe in this place. Lesson learned: bless your children and release them to their life path. They know better than we do. Visit them often, but not too often. They need their space so their wings develop fully. I learned to text once or twice a week with nothing important to say, but just wanted her to know I was thinking of her.

Children are funny little creatures and they turn usually sane adults into crazy and bizarre parents. When it comes to our kids, rationality and moderation goes out the window. We have this insane idea that somehow our children will listen to us because we know everything and want only the very best for them. They can't possibly know that we are so deeply connected to them that our own lives take on a secondary meaning, that our main purpose for living is to become their cheerleading section. They don't know how many times we wake up in the middle of the night filled with stark terror wondering if they are okay, feeling completely helpless to protect them from the dangers of the world. At our very best, we silently love them and ask God to watch over them and then we trust God. There is little more we can constructively do. We know the gauntlet they must run to find their way and carve out a life for themselves and all we can ever do when they leave is pray for them. This may be a good time in our lives to begin to spend more time with God and to let our hearts be open to His wisdom. Maybe we can eke out a small comfort knowing that the Creator of the entire universe is also watching out for our babies.

After our daughter had lived several years in Los Angeles my wife and I worried that she would not get married, would not find the right guy, and then we worried she'd find the wrong guy and would marry him! We mostly worried about all that stuff because that's what parents do. And then one day, our daughter brings him home to meet us and he's perfect! I knew he was perfect even before I met him. Our daughter said he was from Pennsylvania and I thought, "Out of all the men in LA my daughter meets a man from Pennsylvania! I knew from spending time in Harrisburg that anyone from Pennsylvania would be wonderful. They are the salt of the earth." And he was perfect!

Most of us have fond memories of our grandparents, those endearing members of our families that aren't parents, but are like parents. They are the parents of our parents. They appear to be softer and gentler versions of mom and dad. We've spent our whole lives basking in the warmth and radiance of grandma and grandpa, enjoying their doting and indulging. There is something magical about spending time in their home, learning the family traditions and observing that our parents seem to have little or no control over them. In fact, it occurs to us that maybe grandma and grandpa may hold a secret power over our parents that might come in useful to us someday. And now after a lifetime of such memories, my wife and I are on the verge of becoming the legendary grandparents.

When I first met Ayla, I was overwhelmed with pride, tenderness, love, and joy. She took my breath away. One cannot prepare for such a moment. How do we get ready to meet someone that is one hour old? She is fresh from heaven and full of light. I look at my daughter and I look at Ayla and am in state of awe to see how God works, to see the process He set up for us to come into this world. It is such a test of the will to live, the will to be. It is pure, real, physical, and authentic. We are all so connected up in intricate ways we don't understand and cannot comprehend, yet there we are, together…….Life expressing itself! I am consumed by the vision of my daughter and her baby. How can this be? How can something so wonderful be in this place? And then, I remember that it happens at all times and in all places….all the time! Then it hits me…. the homeless guy I saw on the street, the little urchin scrapping out a meager existence is someone's child and my heart breaks with compassion for them that they should be championed, they should be held up to the world as the innocent creatures they are. They should be held in the highest esteem by us all because of who they are as human beings and maybe they didn't have a loving mom or dad back home and maybe they did. But they are here in this place now and just maybe I or you could make a difference in their life.

I think, "how busy and shallow my mind must be to not recognize the little infant child in each one of us and how much grief must God bear for His children as they wander haplessly through this world"? Why are we so despised? Why are we forlorn in this place? Comfort us just a little. Comfort them all for just a little bit. And then the words come to my mind: "I am sending you to those who need me most. Comfort them as best you can. Give them what they need and I will do the rest." There it is, the great commission wrapped up in a few simple words. And so I must do what I can, such as I am, in this place, in this time, to be what God intended me to be. It's a personal message from a personal God. We must be the best human being we can be. We are not more than the pathetic few sent to comfort the suffering among us even as we suffer ourselves. We glean a little light from each one of us and we huddle together in the darkness and pray for the dawn. We ask for the light to come to us and renew us and make us whole. Each breath is a prayer for help, a plea for strength and guidance in the dark of this place.

Ayla's arrival has ushered in a new era of hope for me. I now see the world through a fresh pair of eyes; through a grandpa's eyes and I want the very best world for her. I want her to live in a world where everyone loves each other and where each person is free to develop their full potential as a human being. I now understand that my granddaughter will grow up among all the children of her age. I know how important it is now and has always been that each and every one of us must work each day to make the world a safer and richer place for us all and our children. I want her to walk among the people and be fulfilled. I want the street urchins to be made whole and to be fulfilled. I want God to come back to this place and make His home among us and dry up our tears. I want my granddaughter to be spared the hard choices life demands of us, but I know this will not be so. I know that as she grows up, there will be bumps and bruises, and hard choices for her to make. She will walk into an imperfect world, a world of pain, anguish, loneliness, and suffering. She will need to understand the nature of the human condition and her own condition. I want to make sure she is well equipped to navigate all the hazards of life and to win her dreams for her life.

My hope for her is that wherever she is, she will be surrounded by the love and protection of the church on earth. This is not the buildings and well known cathedrals found around the world. It is not found in the doctrines, dogmas, and traditions of the various denominations found everywhere. It survives and thrives in the hearts and souls of people everywhere that know and comprehend the love of God. The church comes to us in the glance from a stranger and from unexpected help in a time of need. It comes from unlikely places at the right time and might be only a word of encouragement or a brief validation for the next breath we take. It is in these few humble saints that keep the flame of eternal love glowing and bright for those fortunate enough to come in out of the storm and darkness of the 21st century. It has been this way for over two thousand years and continues until this very moment. And now my granddaughter has come to take her place among the saints. For me, this is a blessed moment, a tender moment, and a moment where God lets me see His majesty at work.

Two weeks after this blessed event, I breathe a sigh of relief, a sigh of gratitude that everything turned out so very well, so perfect. It is God's grace flowing through my life and healing old wounds. In another lifetime I went to the hospital with my young wife fully expecting to bring home a baby boy. I was going to be a father so long ago, but unexpected things happened and it was a role I was not meant to play then. Our baby son did not make it. I was 27 years old when I entered the wilderness of pain and anguish. I didn't know why I needed to go there. I didn't know what I had done to deserve the sentence, but it didn't matter, it doesn't matter, and it never matters! Life happens. We get hurt. We bleed out and end up empty.

All that changed with Ayla and her mom. It was the end of my 32 years wandering in the desert. Until that moment, I did not fully understand the meaning that had guided my life for so many years. My daughter did what I could not. She got to have her baby. I could never have seen this image woven into the fabric of my life. I did not know what my past life meant until I saw Ayla, until I saw my daughter have her baby. The whole meaning had been hidden from me for decades. I now have a deeper understanding of God's patient love for us and thanking Him for letting me live to share such a moment. I realize now how totally prepared I was to appreciate the deep tenderness and love such a moment brings. For me, it is a second chance to see a little baby grow up, to be a grandfather to such a lovely child and to watch my awesome daughter blossom into the very best mother in the world. I marvel at how many chances God gives us to see His perfection in our life.

Killing the Jabberwocky

"There exists in the heart of every person, no matter how small, a giant, a champion, that when blessed and released upon the world, will bring a wave of grace and justice if we would but believe it to be true. So many of us are waiting for you to come"-Richard R. Smith

As I look back over my life I realize I'm still exactly the same person I have always been. I'm hopefully a little smarter and certainly more knowledgeable, but basically the same internal character. I'm the same person I've always been from day one. I've approached life from the same angle, the same perspective, and it always feels the same. I realize I've been running the same internal elevator music all my life. It's not good or bad. It just is! It's interesting how our perspective of life changes, but we don't seem to change at all. When we are children, we can't wait to be older because getting older and growing up is what we are supposed to do. We imagine ourselves being older and having the freedom to make our own decisions about everything and getting our shot at living in the fullness of who we are. We feel like we know stuff, but we also know there's a lot of stuff we don't know and well, that's what growing up is all about. Somehow we know the day will come when we will arrive at our destiny and on that day we will know what to do.

Growing up and going through all the different stages I emerged into adulthood without a single clue as to what to do as an adult. I did what everyone else did; I learned to cope. I learned to work, to get along, to study, to encourage the growth, and try to get ahead. Fifty years later I'm still wondering what it's all about. I look around at little children and watch them play at being grown-ups and marvel at their imagination for what they believe their futures will be. I think back to my own childhood and wonder where that guy went to and realize I'm that guy! And then I realize that when you get older, the trick is to learn how to think like a child again, to remember the dreamer and the dream. Life really is very simple, but somehow, somewhere we mixed it all up and made it complicated. We made it boring and difficult as we filled up our time with charts and graphs, schedules, expectations, and a disciplined timetable for all the milestones. We dream up all the grand prizes and then squander everything to win them as if somehow if we don't life won't have any meaning. As adults, we find it hard to go back and become as little children again. In this world it is impossible. In Wonderland all things are possible, even going back in time and experiencing ourselves as children.

From the moment Alice entered Wonderland she began moving toward her destiny, although it didn't seem that way to her. Each encounter along the path in Wonderland yielded another clue from her past, from her previous visit, and ignited an ancient vague memory. Everyone seemed to know her and yet, she had no memory of them. It was odd and peculiar at the same time. Little by little she came to understand that she had been in this place before and had returned for a specific purpose. Eventually she came to realize the nature of her adventure and her role and destiny in the Wonderland story. She came to understand she was the person destined to kill the Jabberwocky and she began to realize that somehow she always knew this to be true. She had only forgotten. There is no one else but her for this task. She was the only one that could wield the sword that would eventually cut off the head of the Jaberwocky and free Wonderland from the oppression of the Red Queen. It was her destiny.

We can't be totally sure that each one of us carries the same singular importance as Alice, yet we know intuitively we have a reach and a touch that is unique in all of life. Our own little world may not be so grand, but it is after all, our world. In much the same way I find myself remembering things from long ago, small pieces of a larger puzzle. I never know quite what they are or where they fit or what they mean, but I save them up anyway, and from time to time, they form a small picture of a much larger mosaic. I'm learning that what I know and understand about myself as a child is still active in me and moving me forward toward whatever manifestation my life is meant to bring to the whole.

We are each called back to our own Wonderland to play the role we were always meant to play. It is a part of the drama of all humankind and it is our little seemingly unimportant part that is reserved only for us. Like Alice we must sooner or later put everything on the line if we are to live out our destiny and become who we were always meant to be. Many of us become confused at the vaguely familiar clues that are there before us and then mixed with our instinctive caution for the thing we fear. We feel it lurking there just out of sight and struggle to decide if it is real or just a dream and we are no longer sure what side of the looking glass we are really on. These are the moments that decide our fate and define the meaning of our life. If we are still asleep in the dream, we miss them altogether.

Sooner or later it comes down to that one thing; we just never know when it will pop up, but when it does, we are either ready to deal with it or we are not. It's happened many times before and we were not ready. We recognize those moments as defeats, as times when we sounded the retreat and left in a hurry so as to not incur any further wounds or damages. But we cannot sustain a full lifetime of defeats without losing all self-respect. There must be some level of process, some social safeguard that defines the bottom for us. At some point, we draw a line in the dirt and make our stand and that point in life usually comes when we understand we have nothing left to lose.

We can start really slow. Take a deep breath. Sit down. Take a nap. Relax. Let time start flowing by without lifting a finger to make it count. Just let it go. It doesn't matter! It doesn't matter now and it never did all those years we've worked ourselves into a frenzy keeping track of the cosmic currency we were collecting to redeem someday. And what did we get for all our effort, for all the trouble and sacrifice? It was a dead end and a life lesson. We got the experience, but that never buys us any prizes worth keeping. What I've learned is: none of the prizes matter a little bit or even at all. They are all worthless trinkets we imagined were important to possess. Somehow we thought we needed them.

I knew all this stuff forty or fifty or even sixty years ago and I forgot! I've been playing the game right along with most everyone else in the world and I bought it all! I'm relearning that life is about living well and the best way to do that is to start right now where I'm at. When I start here, I'm starting at bedrock. I have a firm foundation on which to stand. I can go no lower. There is nothing left to lose. One of the main lessons I had to learn was that all the meaning in life was always right inside me. I had it all along, but believed it was out there somewhere and I had to go and find it.

I had to return to Wonderland. I had to learn to be a child again to gain perspective on what was happening to me in my life now. It slowly began to dawn on me how growing up changed me in ways I didn't realize or intend. I did not venture that far from home when I was swept away by all that glitters and my destiny was set. I became a new creation and one that I thought the world wanted. It wasn't me, only my creation, but I knew that, sort of. It would take decades of wandering through the wasteland of illusions and delusions before I could finally return home.

My experience cannot be singular and solitary. There must be others out there, the foolish others like myself, that experienced life this way. Fact is I believe this happens to most of us. It's really true that the best things in life are free. They were there all along, but we did not honor them for what they are. The world for us is not more than our country, our state, our city, and mainly, our family. It is in the family structure that we are born, nurtured, and blossom into what we will become. But it doesn't stop there. It only returns there someday with interest if we have the courage, the strength, the stamina, and the will to return home again. I have none of these qualities, but I have a new granddaughter and now I must go home and take my place in her family structure.

I want to share a secret with you; when we live in the present moment as our authentic selves, our presence gives others around us permission to access and reveal their authentic selves. When we do this, it reinforces our authentic self and we grow stronger together. Our authentic presence gives us permission to open up the secret chamber in our heart where we placed our true selves so long ago. Your authentic presence gives me permission to open my secret chamber. When this happens, a tiny key will open a tiny lock and the universe reveals itself to us all and allows a small yet brilliant stream of light to flood into the darkness of human misunderstanding. When you do this people all around you will be attracted to the light coming from you. The bible says, *"The light has come into the darkness and the darkness has not overcome it."* You will no longer need faith for you will immediately have knowledge of God. You will instantly understand the parable of the pearl of great price for you will have found your own pearl of great price. You will have rediscovered your real and authentic self. You will never lose it again at any cost. That's why enlightened people so willingly die for what they believe. They cannot bear to live without it. They have experienced the truth and nothing less than the truth will ever do again. The illusions and delusions of this world no longer have any power to sway or convince us to deviate from the path we are now on.

There is something novel and pure about living in a human body, being focused in physical form for a period in time to experience self-existence, to experience our self apart from God for a time and then to reconnect with Him in grace and to contemplate the journey in between. We have to get ourselves to the edge of the precipice where we can see that we can actually jump off into the oblivion of real spiritual order and escape the chaos of the human condition. We need to come to a point of understanding where the absurd becomes the possible, where dreams come true, so there is a real need for some level of faith. We have to know we are worth it and can somehow survive the fall. It only requires a little faith and what's a little faith compared to the years of grinding boredom and dead ends we've already experienced?

The answer was always deep inside me. It has always been there, but I chose to believe everyone else. I esteemed everyone else above my own gut feeling and self-worth and denied my own personal reality as somehow inferior and untrue. Why is it so hard to develop a rock solid confidence in my own gut feelings? When I see the color of the night sky in winter and detect the different hues of blue that look really inky black, I see something bigger than me. I see a sky painted by the infinite. When I take the time to watch the sun come up over the mountains and brighten the valley, there is a communion of action that includes me in the unfolding events of the day. This is when I see myself as part of something bigger than I think I am. This is the universe looking back on itself. This is as good as it gets. Finding your true self is not an easy task. It is a difficult and dangerous journey. All the dangers and difficulties were crafted by us long ago when we hid ourselves from ourselves. We don't even remember this, which is another clever tool we devised to make the mystery complete and insure we'd never go poking around there again, ever! But there we are and there we'll stay hidden until we decide it's worth the risk to get to the truth of ourselves.

What I found when this happened to me is nearly impossible to describe. People speak of the ineffability of the spiritual experience that it is beyond words to accurately describe. I fully agree and yet must attempt some kind of description. I strongly suspect when I discovered my real self, that I was seeing my reflection in my mother's eyes the very first time she saw me and maybe the same reflection for many times after that. It was my first experience of myself in human form breathing on my own and being held by another human being that loved me for myself and without any conditions. I was a body from her body. My mother's body and my father's body created me, but my mother's body grew me. She must have looked with wonderment and awe at her new baby. That's how it felt for me to see my real self. When I saw my granddaughter for the very first time when she was only one hour old, I was struck with wonderment and awe and a deep abiding sense of unconditional love for this little child that had done nothing except show up in my life. Her little presence brought me to my knees and made me instantly understand how big God really is and how much He loves us all. My whole family was wrapped in this cosmic blanket of unconditional love where nothing is ever lost, where grief never comes, and where we must all end up forever and ever. There are no words in this place, only the meanings of things. You don't learn here, you simply know and understand. It is a place of sublime peace and comfort with an overriding sense you belong there and belong no place else. It is home. It is my home and your home. It is the Heaven God promises.

Looking into my granddaughter's eyes for the first time and every time since, I am struck by a crystal clear moment out of time where my whole past comes into clear focus and I can connect every experience in my life into a single fabric of being that brought me to this very present moment, to understand, to behold, to be captivated by the gaze of a baby and see God looking in on me and my little life. That's how He does it! If I hadn't gone to Vietnam, if my son hadn't died, if I hadn't wandered the earth for twenty years as an empty shell, if I hadn't walked away from the church and then crawled back again years later, if I hadn't suffered nights of terror being divorced from myself…..if I hadn't died a thousand times, if I hadn't railed against all that is against me and fought back and finally surrendered……I would not fully understand the meaning of the redemption coming from this little baby's eyes and drink it into my parched soul and be reborn into a new human being, a new grandpa! I am overwhelmed with gratitude at being here.

This astonishing experience is available to us all anytime we are ready. I learned about it last May when I attended a two-day seminar called "The Wow Factor". Those two days transformed my life from dying to living to being. Since then I've spent all my free time reading and learning about what happened to me, how it happened, and what I could do to make it happen all the time for everyone. It is nothing less than the pot of gold at the end of the rainbow and the meaning of life and the meaning of our self in this crazy world. I now understand it and how to do it and want to encourage everyone to try it and see for yourself, discover your real self.

What I've discovered and now understand is that my mother's eyes gave me my identity, showed me who I was, who I am. At some point in life, most people didn't look at me that way and I changed. I learned how to get what I wanted from people a different way and I put down the real me to keep the more effective false me. We learn at an early age to become cleaver and crafty manipulators of those around us. It always works like a charm, but there is a dear price we all must pay for the service. We hide our real selves from us in a place we will never willingly look again and we forget the whole thing. If you will find 2-3 people to sit with you and do nothing more than stare into each other's eyes for about five minutes without laughing, smiling or talking, but only having warm positive thoughts about the person you are seeing in front of you, at some point, you will see their authentic self, and if you keep looking, at some point, you will see your own authentic self-reflected in their eyes. It's the same look we all got when we were born. This exercise, if done correctly, creates unconditional love. It allows the truth to exist in you and around you and between you and the others. When you do this, you won't want to do anything else. You will understand who you are and why you are here on earth. You will begin to understand the value of your own gifts and the need to be strong and have the courage and faith to share those gifts with anyone and everyone. When you give your gifts to others you will be giving them permission to give their gifts as well. You will shine your light into their darkness and be there to watch them discover their own gifts. And so it goes. It's the circle of life, the secret of life and it's free!

I've learned to look for myself between each breath. In the moments before I inhale and the moment before I exhale, there I am! It is a single point of being, a snapshot in time. It appears to happen so quickly I never noticed it before. Again and again and again, there I am! I have no expectation other than to see myself before me for what I am. The second I get the idea that I'm somebody with something to do, everything changes. As the moments run together they begin to create a movie of me moving through time just like the way photographs when viewed in rapid succession becomes a movie. It is the illusion of time streaming by, of time moving, as if it existed at all. I have shifted from doing to being and now I'm defined no longer by what I do, but who I am.

From the perspective of a singular moment of awareness I see maybe for the first time, how ragged the fabric of everything really is. I had believed it was real. All objects must be perceived as having a meaning, a purpose, and being a small part of a greater picture. The mind connects the dots, draws conclusions, and runs off in search of fame and glory with our ego. The real me is left only in the small space that exists between each breath, to be.

What I've learned about finding my authentic self is that it is the jumping off point for my faith. The church believes and Christians will tell you that if you just believe in Jesus, just invite Him into your life that somehow magically He will appear and everything will be better. It's not quite that simple. It's not a magic trick. God is not a magic trick and neither is Jesus and Christianity is not some hocus pocus spiritual sideshow. The Holy Spirit has more respect for you than to invade the one place He set up for you to be you. If you take it seriously, if you study a little bit, you will understand that your faith, which is free, will cost you everything. You cannot go through the eye of the needle as a whole being. You cannot take up the pearl of great price and keep all your other crap as well. You cannot waltz into heaven with all your bling and other ideas about life. Being a Christian, a committed Christian and going the distance strips you of everything, but the prize is so much worth the trade. When you are reunited with your authentic self, the theology will take care of itself. You can draw your own conclusions about God, life, and the universe.

Sooner or later you find yourself hanging on a cross, naked and bleeding and somehow it's okay. Somehow it is worth it to give up everything you ever thought you were to pick up everything God made you to be. The trade is a no-brainer, but most people won't take the time to consider their option. If you want to find out how it all turns out, just check out the New Testament and find out how things turned out for Jesus and his disciples. Almost all of them were murdered like Jesus and they all went willingly to their death. Jesus conquered death. He conquered death in the body, the same body you and I have. He did it once for all of us. The Son of God led the way first and came back and told us. He appeared to his followers and showed them his wounds. God gave us Jesus as payment for our sins and as the promise of His eternal love for us. What more could we ask for?

The church has it wrong when they try to sell you on the idea of Jesus. They think they're doing what they're supposed to. They are well-meaning, but the social mind today is much different than it was thousands of years ago. Our minds are completely skeptical, absorbed into a singular selfishness. They should be helping you find your authentic self, the self God made you to be. When you find that person, you will know God and you won't need someone to guide you through the experience. You will be there yourself. You will get your instructions directly and you will want to be in community with other believers.

I realize now that I don't have any special skills. I know a lot of stuff, but I'm not really good at any one thing. I've learned my role in this life is to help people find their "on" switch and step through the threshold of a world of infinite possibilities. My job is to open the door, to be inviting and helpful, and let people in, to invite them in, and to drag them in if I have to. How do I know this for sure? When I was in the first grade we all had to use crayons to draw pictures. When I drew the best picture I could draw, I looked around and everyone else's drawing was better than mine. Mine wasn't bad. It just wasn't as good as everyone else's. I could see by their use of color and form they had a keener insight into the object of the lesson than I did. Their drawing skills were better than mine. I knew right then I was a helper. I knew that I knew this. I understood immediately the role I was meant to play in my life. God sent me to be a helper to all the doers in the world. We need more doers. I hope my words have helped you find yourself. We need you to show up and show us what you can do. You are the One! Amen! Namaste!

P.S.

Let me hear from you. You can reach me at the following sites:

Richard@RichardRSmith.com

Richardrsmith1@twitter.com

Ephphata@tumblr.com

Other books by Richard R. Smith

"Lunch with Dr. Frankenstein"

"Hyperion Rising"- coming in summer of 2014

Bibliography

"The Drama of the Gifted Child" by Alice Miller, Perseus Book Group, Copyright 1981 by Basic Books, Inc. ISBN- 978-0-465-01261-9

A Course in Miracles Copyright @ Foundation for Inner Peace 1975, 1985, 1992, 1996. All rights reserved. Second edition by Viking Penguin, a division of Penguin Books USA Inc.

ISBN- 0-670-86975-9

RSV Old Testament, copyrighted 1952, © 1973, 1980 By the Division of Christian Education of the National Council of the Churches of Christ in the U.S.A

RSV New Testament, copyrighted 1946, © 1971, 1973 By the Division of Christian Education of the National Council of the Churches of Christ in the U.S.A

The sayings of Lao Tzu

The sayings of Buddha

Suggested Reading

The following books were essential reading for me while writing my book. I highly recommend any and all of them to my readers as source material.

"For Your Own Good" by Alice Miller, Farrar Straus & Giroux

"Ethics" by Dietrich Bonhoeffer Macmillan Publishing

"The Time of the Assassins" by Henry Miller New Directions Publishing

"A Return to Love" by Marianne Williamson Harper Collins Publishing

"Man's Search for Meaning" by Viktor Frankl Pocket Books-Simon & Schuster

"God, Power, And Evil: A Process Theodicy" by David Griffin Westminster John Knox Press

www.ingramcontent.com/pod-product-compliance
Lightning Source LLC
Chambersburg PA
CBHW061942070426
42450CB00007BA/1027